THE
GARDENS
OF
ENGLAND

Treasures of the National Gardens Scheme

THE GARDENS OF ENGLAND

Treasures of the National Gardens Scheme

Edited by
George Plumptre
Preface by Joe Swift

Foreword by
HRH The Prince of Wales

MERRELL
LONDON · NEW YORK

CLARENCE HOUSE

The National Gardens Scheme is a unique movement which has had the most profound effect on our relationship with gardening over a great many decades. By combining the joy of garden visiting with fund-raising for good causes, it has created a self-sustaining national movement that, every year, encourages more gardeners to share the fruits of their labours and helps more visitors enjoy some of the most beautiful gardens in the country.

It is extraordinary to think that this movement grew out of nothing more than a one-year project to support district nurses. This wonderful book brings this story to life and I hope it brings as much joy to those who read it as the gardens do to those who visit them.

Preface

Joe Swift

As a TV presenter, writer and President of the NGS I travel up and down the country quite a lot visiting gardens, meeting garden owners and having plenty of fun as I go. I'm a lucky man and I know it. The TV programmes help to show people gardens they may not be able get to, and also, I hope, inspire some to garden themselves. Watching TV and visiting a garden oneself, however, are two very different things. To experience a garden at first hand, to walk and be drawn through it as its maker intended, taking in every angle and smelling whatever is on offer along the way, simply cannot be beaten, and it's what garden visiting is all about. As well as the garden speaking for itself, the personality of its maker will be stamped all over the plot, and when you add the setting – be it rural, suburban or urban – the garden's aspect and conditions, and the precise palette of plants grown, the result can only be a one-off. Every single NGS garden is unique, and of course they are all constantly changing with the seasons and maturing over time. I have gone back to gardens years after my first visit, or during a different season, and learned so much from that revisit that I now know that no garden, however iconic, can really ever be 'ticked off' the list. This is good news. It proves that there's more than a lifetime's worth of garden visiting ahead of us all, and with every NGS garden visited, important money is raised for our beneficiaries along the way.

Garden Visiting and
The National Gardens Scheme

George Plumptre

Garden visiting had been evolving for many centuries when, rather by chance, an organization emerged during the 1920s in England and Wales that brought about a revolution in this social pastime. As in the case of most things to do with gardens since the Middle Ages, it was those of the Italian Renaissance that had been the first to attract visitors, during the early sixteenth century. Not long after that, it was recorded that Philip II of Spain (always keen to know what his enemies were up to) sent his court draughtsman, Anthonis van den Wyngaerde, to visit and record details of the gardens of the Tudor royal palaces, and English gardens have attracted curious visitors ever since.

During the reign of Elizabeth I, lavish creations, intended to impress the queen, such as her favourite the Earl of Leicester's new garden at his home, Kenilworth Castle in Warwickshire, were keenly inspected by aristocratic visitors. At the beginning of the seventeenth century the Renaissance brilliance of the gardens created by the Herbert family around their Wiltshire home, Wilton House, was particularly popular. During the Civil War, the diarist and horticulturalist John Evelyn brightened up his years of exile in France by visiting some of the new gardens being created there; his expeditions to various English gardens on his return home after the Restoration of Charles II in 1660 were joined by other now well-known travellers, such as Celia Fiennes, who recorded their visits to houses and gardens in diaries.

The most significant boost to garden visiting came in eighteenth-century England, when appreciating gardens became a visible sign of 'good taste', and when the relationship between gardens and the natural landscape turned into a philosophical one. Garden visiting became an increasingly widespread social pastime, as Charles Quest-Ritson has described: 'Taste was now one of the accomplishments of polite society – an ability to make value judgements on matters of art, architecture, furniture, gardens and natural scenery' (*The English Garden: A Social History*, 2001). One garden, Stowe in Buckinghamshire, led the way as a destination for visitors. Its aristocratic owner, Lord Cobham (a member of the political elite), and the involvement of a succession of leading figures in the development of the English landscape garden – Charles Bridgeman, John Vanbrugh, William Kent and Lancelot 'Capability' Brown – gave it an immediately stellar reputation. Its status was confirmed in 1744, when the first ever guidebook about a single garden, *Description of the Gardens of Lord Viscount Cobham at Stowe*, was published.

One of the first visitors to Stowe to record his impression had been Lord Perceval, in a letter of 1717 to his brother-in-law Daniel Dering. Clearly he did not think much of the accommodation offered by Lord Cobham: 'In my last I told you the good Stomach my wife had at Stow my Ld Cobham's Inn, and gave you a journal of her health till Wednesday night. Our Inn was a scurvy one and had not beds for all. Those of us who went to bed could not sleep for fleas and gnats.' But he was impressed with what he had really come to see: 'The Gardens, by reason of the good contrivance of the walks[,] seem to be three times as large as they are … You think twenty times you have no more to see, and of a sudden find yourself in some new garden or walk as finish'd and adorn'd as that you left. Nothing is more irregular in the whole, nothing more regular in the parts, which totally differ one from another.'

A few years later, in 1738, an anonymous account suggests that the popularity of the Stowe gardens had led to a formalization of arrangements for visitors: 'The entrance into the Gardens is at the End of a long but Narrow Visto, leading up to the front of the House. On Each side of it are Two Porticos of Stone on Ionick Pillars. A Bell hanging on the Wall of the Garden being rung, the Gardiner who attends on Purpose conducts you up a little Ascent till you arrive at the Platform of it.'

During the eighteenth century, Stowe and the other most fashionable gardens of the day showed clear evidence of popularity, and, as was the case with many gatherings during this ebullient age, things occasionally got out of hand. Daniel Defoe in the 1720s reported that Lord Tylney's gardens at Wanstead were so popular with sightseers that he was 'obliged to restrain his servants from shewing them' (*Tour Through the Eastern Counties of England*, 1722). The famous diarist Horace Walpole decided that the only way to cope with the large number of visitors to his Gothick home, Strawberry Hill in Twickenham, was to enforce a system of pre-booked tickets. He noted in a letter to his vicar that Philip Southcote had to close Woodburn Farm to visitors because the 'savages who came as connoisseurs scribbled a thousand brutalities in the buildings' (16 June 1781). Henry Hoare, the owner of the picturesque landscape idyll of Stourhead in Wiltshire (second in reputation only to Stowe), was constrained to

Stowe in Buckinghamshire became the most famous landscape garden of the eighteenth century and was celebrated in a series of early guidebooks about English gardens, including *The Beauties of Stow* (1750) by George Bickham.

build a hotel to accommodate the hoards of curious visitors who came to see the garden. And at his *ferme ornée*, The Leasowes in Warwickshire, William Shenstone found it necessary to caution the 'Sunday starers' in one of the engraved inscriptions along his circuit walk: 'And tread with awe these favour'd bowers, Nor wound the shrubs, nor bruise the flowers; So may your path with sweets abound, So may your couch with rest be crown'd! But harm betide the wayward swain, Who dares our hallow'd haunts profane.'

If during the eighteenth century garden visiting had become fashionable for the well-to-do, during the nineteenth it was to become first a recommended pastime for the growing middle classes and then, with the advent of cheap rail travel, accessible to huge numbers of the urban working classes. The popularization of domestic gardening had begun in the eighteenth century with the mass distribution of nurserymen's catalogues, but it was restricted in practical terms by the primitive housing conditions most people endured. By the mid-nineteenth century the concept of the ideal English home (however small) as a house with a garden was both attractive and attainable by a slowly increasing percentage of the population. The *Gardener's Magazine*, first published in 1826 by the tireless popularizer of gardens John Loudon, became the first mass-market gardening magazine, and, on occasions, highlighted the benefits of garden visiting; the author of one article suggested that getting out and looking at other gardens was better than consulting a book.

Most significantly, hand-in-hand with the development of public parks in the burgeoning industrial towns and cities of northern England came the idea that to visit a garden or park was an agreeable recreational activity, relaxing and good for the health, both mental and physical. In 1843 Joseph Paxton designed the first public park in the world, for the Merseyside town of Birkenhead, and during subsequent decades public parks became essential elements of town planning. The example set in Birkenhead was followed in Europe and the United States, not least by Frederick Law Olmsted – the 'father' of landscape design in America – who laid out New York's Central Park and parks in Boston and other American cities. After visiting Birkenhead, where he took detailed notes, Olmsted wrote: 'And all this magnificent pleasure-ground is entirely, unreservedly, and for ever the people's own. The poorest British peasant is as free to enjoy it in all its parts, as the British queen' (*Walks and Talks of an American Farmer in England*, 1852).

Paxton also made significant alterations to the historic gardens of Chatsworth House in Derbyshire, where he was head gardener from 1826 to 1858, including the addition of a number of spectacular features for the amazement of visitors. In September 1867 *The Gardener* magazine

North West View of the Inn at Stourton.

described the Whitsun holiday at Chatsworth: 'The park and grounds were swarming with holiday makers, for it was one of England's great holidays, Whit-Monday. Here were little pale-faced men and women from the cotton factories of Manchester, dark denizens of the Staffordshire potteries, and the sharp, active-looking mechanics of Leeds, Bradford and Halifax, all brought hither in special trains' (p. 347). What a happy coincidence that sixty years later the National Gardens Scheme (NGS) would be launched on the Whitsun holiday weekend.

By the turn of the twentieth century the activity of garden visiting had developed in a unique way in Britain because of the factors it was acknowledged to combine: aesthetic pleasure; the appreciation of artistic quality and excellence in horticulture and garden design; education; recreation; recuperation; and curiosity. All contributed to the idea that visiting a garden was an agreeable and worthy occupation. But beyond urban public parks, the places accessible to prospective visitors were still restricted to a relatively small number of almost exclusively famous gardens around great houses.

In her introduction to *Garden Open Today* by Alison Rix, a book published in 1987 to celebrate sixty years of the NGS, Rachel Crawshay, the scheme's Organizing Secretary at the time, wrote: 'Despite its title, it was the care of people rather than the care of plants that led to the creation of the National Gardens Scheme.' It would not have been expected that the death in 1925 of Queen Alexandra, the widow of King Edward VII, would have an impact on the development of garden visiting in England. However, the queen had been a much-loved and devoted champion of nurses; in 1902 she founded Queen Alexandra's Imperial Military Nursing Service to look after servicemen wounded during the second Boer War, and that organization developed into the modern military nursing services of today.

One year earlier, after the death of Queen Victoria, Alexandra had taken over the position of patron of the Jubilee Congress of District Nursing (now the Queen's Nursing Institute) from her mother-in-law. Victoria, who had given her patronage to the organization in 1887 as part of her Golden Jubilee celebrations, had supported it since its foundation in Liverpool in 1859 by William Rathbone. Rathbone was a wealthy Liverpool businessman and philanthropist who, having employed a nurse to look after his terminally ill wife, commissioned the nurse to look after people living in the Liverpool slums. Quickly realizing that the task was far beyond what one person could achieve, Rathbone began funding the small group that grew into the first body of district nurses.

In order to mark Alexandra's death, the governing council of the organization decided to launch a memorial fund, to provide a capital resource for their support of district nurses, and to finance a

The principle of public access to 'green spaces' – parks and gardens – was championed by Joseph Paxton. He designed the first public park at Birkenhead in Lancashire; its boathouse and plan with distinctive serpentine paths are shown here.

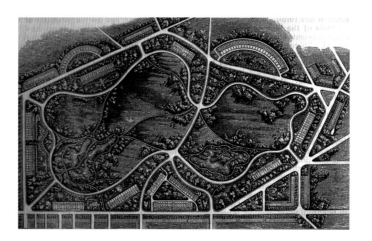

'visible memorial' to the late queen. At a meeting in 1926 of the memorial committee, one of the members who was also a council member of the institute, a Miss Elsie Wagg, is reported to have suggested: 'We've got all these beautiful gardens in this country and hardly anyone sees them except the owners and their friends – why don't we ask some of them to open next year for the Appeal?' Thus the National Gardens Scheme was born.

Looking back, it was an extraordinary effort, a testament to not only the determination but also the social contacts of those involved. Within a few months, the owners of 349 properties with gardens all over England and Wales – from the grandest ducal stately homes to impressive country houses and more modest establishments – had all agreed to open their gardens to visitors on a date of their choice during June 1927. Not surprisingly perhaps, since the scheme was being launched to contribute to the fund in memory of his mother, King George V agreed to open the garden at Sandringham House in Norfolk, always his mother's favourite residence and her home for the last few years of her life.

Equally significantly, the fledgling scheme was guaranteed support by two of the most influential publications of the day, *The Times* newspaper and *Country Life* magazine. On 10 March 1927 *The Times* carried the first public announcement of the scheme under the headline 'National Memorial to Queen Alexandra':

A scheme which will appeal to garden lovers is being started by the women's committee of the National Memorial to Queen Alexandra all over England and Wales … During the Whitsuntide holiday, from May 30 to June 11 inclusive, owners are being asked to open their gardens at a small charge. The owners are responding generously, and soon it is hoped to announce a full list of the gardens and the facilities for visiting them.

True to its word, within a few weeks the paper published the first of a series of lists of the participating gardens and their opening dates, produced regularly throughout the summer. It proved to be crucial publicity. Originally there were to have been nearly 350 gardens opening in June, but early indications were so encouraging that before the first garden had opened it had been decided to extend the scheme through July and August, by the end of which month 609 gardens had opened.

Logistically the organization of the garden openings was supremely impressive. A committee of women was mobilized to ensure a succession of open days throughout the three months. Many owners decided to turn their open day into a real occasion: bands played and lavish teas were served. To remind everyone what it was all in aid of, district nurses visited many of the gardens in their uniforms. One stroke of organizing genius

Below
Chatsworth House in Derbyshire, where Paxton built the largest glass building in the world – the great Conservatory (demolished *c.* 1920) – was one of the first privately owned gardens to admit visitors on public holidays.

Below, right
William Rathbone, who founded the district nursing movement in his native Liverpool in 1859.

was the decision for all gardens to charge the same entrance fee, one shilling, thus greatly simplifying both the message and the accounting of funds raised. By the middle of June an article in *Country Life* was celebrating the achievement: 'In whatever part of the country one may live, the gates of the finest gardens will be open … June on an English lawn with the scent of English flowers, in the sun, is the most real pleasure of all.'

But it was the piece in *The Times* on 31 May 1927 recording the very first openings, which had taken place over the Whitsun weekend, that highlighted the real social revolution offered by the scheme – equal access for all:

Among the gardens one could visit yesterday were those of Hatfield House … If experience at Hatfield should prove to be general, as there is no reason to doubt, this experiment will be successful from all points of view. Those who went to Hatfield by motor-car were allowed to drive through the gates right up to the house, and having paid a shilling to a boy at a table, could wander where they liked … The gates were open from 11 o'clock until 7 but there was no intention of shutting them on the stroke of the hour if people were still coming in. It was hoped locally that Hatfield's contribution to the fund would be £20 but that was a good deal to expect so early in the scheme.

Previously, unrestricted access to all had been offered only by the public gardens and parks created since the mid-nineteenth century, especially in the north of England, to allow recreation and leisure in green spaces for the swelling ranks of the urban working classes. Visitors to private gardens were almost invariably subjected to some kind of selection or vetting, and in many cases access was effectively by invitation only. Now, whether at Hatfield – the home of the Marquess of Salisbury, a member of the government of the day and son of a prime minister – or at any of the other great establishments, entry was for anyone, regardless of their social rank, as long as they paid their contribution to charity. It was a landmark in social equality.

The organizers did not simply rely on visitors turning up on the day, as was confirmed by another piece in *The Times* at about the same time:

In order to enable garden-lovers to take advantage of the opportunity of visiting gardens at some distance from their own homes, comprehensive tours have been organized to most counties. From London it will be possible to visit nearly 100 famous gardens in the south and west of England by motor Pullman coaches … The inclusive charges cover the cost of the motor tours, hotel accommodation, entrance fees to gardens and gratuities.

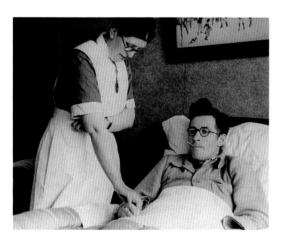

During the 1920s, when the National Gardens Scheme was founded, care at home by district nurses was a vital part of national healthcare.

Before the end of June, with two months of garden opening still to come, the success of the scheme was clear to all. As a result, the momentous decision was made to continue in subsequent years what had been launched as a one-year contribution to a memorial fund, as recorded again in *The Times*, on 27 June 1927:

Suggestions have been made from many quarters that the scheme should be made an annual one, and after consideration it has now been decided to make a permanent use of the organization created for this purpose by creating a rota of gardens year by year which might, by the permission of their owners, be open to the public for the purpose of benefiting the national work of the Queen's Institute of District Nursing.

The institute set up what was first known as the Gardens of England and Wales Scheme, managed by a committee with Hilda, Duchess of Richmond as the first chairman. Not surprisingly, Elsie Wagg was also on the committee, along with representatives of the Royal Horticultural Society and *Country Life*. In an early indication of the formidable devotion to the scheme shown by many of its leading figures over the years, the Duchess of Richmond remained as chairman for twenty years, and was a committed supporter until her death in 1971, just short of her 100th birthday.

In its first sixty years, there were only four different chairmen of the scheme.

When the last garden closed its gates in 1927, the money raised totalled some £8000, which meant that, at one shilling each, about 160,000 people had visited – in many cases accompanied by children, who, as today, were allowed in free. Not only did this augur well for the future fund-raising potential of the scheme, but also it suddenly shed light on the extraordinary popularity of garden visiting. During the next few years, well-known gardens that had not opened in the first year joined the scheme; it was as though, if one were fortunate enough to own an admired garden, one had an obligation to open it for a day in support of the scheme. Hidcote in Gloucestershire first took part in 1928 and Sissinghurst, Kent, in 1930, then under the ownership of their respective creators, Lawrence Johnston and Vita Sackville-West with her husband, Harold Nicolson. Today, both gardens continue to open for the scheme under the ownership of the National Trust (Sissinghurst appears on pp. 66–69).

In 1930 the first complete guide to the gardens opening in the coming year was published for the scheme by *Country Life*. So began a tradition that developed after the Second World War, with the advent of the distinctive covers in 1949, into *The Yellow Book*. With the outbreak of war most gardens, inevitably, were not able to continue opening. But a number did: active support for

Lavish walled gardens with large teams of gardeners were still a feature of English estates between the wars, and were typical of gardens opening for the NGS in its first years.

*Nothing could be more useful to the amateur gardener than to observe other people's ideas, other people's successes, and other people's failures. ...
One could go and sit in those gardens on a summer evening, and imagine what one's own garden (and one's life) might be.*

Vita Sackville-West, *In Your Garden* (1951)

district nurses through the war years, when they were making a considerable contribution, was universally popular; and the enjoyment of garden visiting itself was deemed to be good for morale. On a more practical note, it was felt that many of the gardens would provide valuable examples of how to grow vegetables to help sustain the war effort.

Not surprisingly, a major decision about the future of the scheme was made in 1948 with the establishment of the National Health Service. In theory, the new health service meant that district nurses no longer had to rely on charitable donations; however, the institute remained intact as their organizing body, and, as a result, it was deemed appropriate – not least because of its popularity – to continue the annual scheme raising funds from garden opening.

The scheme continued to be run as part of the Queen's Nursing Institute (QNI) until 1979, by which time the annual 'yellow book' had been titled *Gardens in England and Wales Open for Charity*. But in that year it was decided that because the scheme had become so successful at fund-raising it should be given its own identity, and in 1980 the National Gardens Scheme Charitable Trust was founded. Nursing and caring would continue to be the principal beneficiaries, but not necessarily only as practised by district nurses and the QNI; in 1984 funds were given to the first new beneficiary, Macmillan Cancer Support (then

known as the National Society for Cancer Relief). Ten years later the umbrella of support was widened to include the other major cancer nursing charity, Marie Curie Cancer Care, as well as the hospice movement in the form of the charity Help the Hospices, and the more recently recognized needs of carers supported by the charity Crossroads Care (which, since its merger with the Princess Royal Trust for Carers in 2012, has become Carers Trust). In 1986 the garden-opening operation Gardener's Sunday was taken on by the scheme, and the Gardeners' Royal Benevolent Society (now Perennial) became a regular beneficiary.

It would be fair to say that even as late as 1980, when the NGS emerged as an independent charitable entity, the gardens that opened in support of the scheme were similar in type to those that had opened in the early years: those attached to country houses – or, at least, houses in a village or rural setting – with an emphasis on horticultural excellence and a very high standard of maintenance and appearance. In the three decades or so that have followed, not only has the total number of gardens opening increased roughly threefold, from 1250 to 3800, but also the variety of gardens has blossomed.

Small gardens have been the most notable introduction, and there is no better indication of this than a study of gardens opening in Greater London. When Penny Snell, the present chairman

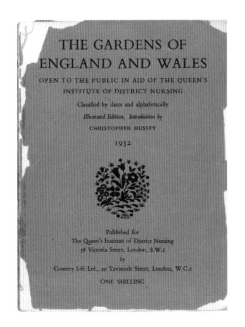

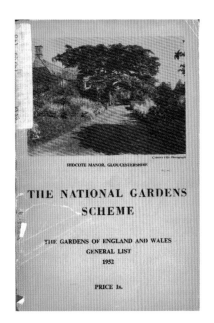

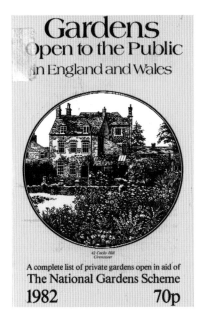

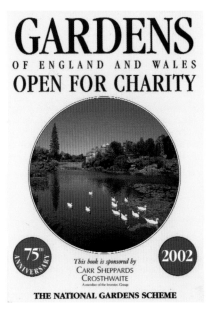

The evolving front covers of the National Gardens Scheme's annual guide, first published in 1930 and known throughout the post-war decades as *The Yellow Book*.

of the NGS, took over as the scheme's County Organizer for London in 1983, there were some thirty gardens opening in her area; today there are nearly 250. Equally important has been the number of gardens opening as groups, whether scattered through a village or all in the same street of a town or city. Their attractions are fascinatingly different from those of large gardens, and have greatly enriched what the scheme has to offer visitors.

As the size and style of gardens opening in support of the scheme have changed, so too has what visitors are looking for. Education about plants and ideas for garden design, often enriched by conversation with the garden's owner or gardener, will always be in high demand. But organic and environmental, sustainable values and examples of their good practice are the priorities for many of today's visiting audience; as are simple peace and solitude or somewhere to enjoy with a family. In a fascinating reminder of the war years, when one of the priorities was opening gardens that demonstrated the growing of fresh vegetables, visitors seek out those gardens that have good examples of fruit and vegetable cultivation – even on a small scale, perhaps in pots and other containers.

The variety of gardens has been further expanded by the introduction of other particular types, such as allotment groups, the gardens of primary schools and even a prison garden. But without doubt, one of the scheme's most potent attractions remains the fact that the great majority of its gardens are privately owned and not accessible at any other time. For many potential visitors, the one Sunday afternoon a year that a certain garden can be visited becomes an opportunity to satisfy curiosity as well as a chance for an enjoyable gardening experience.

Garden visiting has evolved over many centuries from being a pastime for the travelling elite to being politely fashionable for the middle classes, a source of relaxation for the working classes and, finally, a true harbinger of democracy with the advent of unrestricted visiting for all. Similarly, the NGS has evolved through more than eight decades, to present a definitive picture of gardens in Britain, how they have changed and the trends, fashions and priorities that have emerged, and to respond subtly to the changing tastes and aspirations of the visiting audience. Two constants have provided a foundation for the scheme's charitable contributions: the generosity and hard work of owners and their gardeners, who open their gates (and commit considerable resources in preparation); and the enjoyment of visitors who follow the yellow arrows to make a discovery, happy in the knowledge that their enjoyment will bring real benefit to others.

Three examples of the rich variety of smaller gardens that have joined the scheme in the most recent decades: Brynteg in Glamorgan (far left), Matara Meditative Gardens in Gloucestershire (left) and Michaelmas in Hampshire.

1927–39
Gardening in the Jazz Age

Elspeth Napier

From an economic standpoint, the years between the wars were gloomy, with the General Strike in 1926 and the Wall Street crash of 1929 casting a blight on activities. In the 1930s the north of England, and especially its industry, suffered more than the south, where many white-collar jobs were being created and millions of new homes built, all with their rectangular front and back gardens.

In gardening, we can see both an end to and the beginning of fashions. Three giants of Edwardian times – William Robinson, Gertrude Jekyll and Ellen Willmott – died in the 1930s, and the all-powerful head gardeners of Victorian days gradually faded away. The building of new homes led to an increasing interest in gardening, although the new householders were not knowledgeable; the BBC saw the demand and started making gardening programmes in the 1920s. At first, Mrs Marion Cran (an amateur) broadcast once a fortnight, but in 1931 she was replaced by Mr C.H. Middleton (a professional), and he was soon broadcasting

regularly on Sunday afternoons. From 1936 he also presented a television series, but that lasted only until the beginning of the Second World War.

There were several magazines to help the new gardeners. *Amateur Gardening, Popular Gardening* and *Gardening Illustrated* had all been started in the nineteenth century. Two new magazines were published, *My Garden: An Intimate Magazine for Garden Lovers* and *New Flora & Silva* (for the serious gardener), but neither had the staying power of the earlier ones. *A Concise Dictionary of Gardening*, by the editor of *Amateur Gardening*, was published in 1937, and the Royal Horticultural Society (RHS) was in the process of compiling its *Dictionary of Gardening* (eventually published in 1951).

In 1928 the RHS organized a conference on landscape architecture that resulted in the foundation of a professional institute in 1929 (it is now known as the Landscape Institute).

Rockeries, which had been built in Victorian times and earlier and became fashionable in large

gardens in the early twentieth century, spread in the interwar years to the new suburban gardens. The Alpine Garden Society was formed in 1929, and its equivalent in Scotland in 1933, and the Rock Bank flourished at the Chelsea Flower Show. In the 1930s Constance Spry was transforming the art of flower arrangement in 'Society', and this trend spread after the war through the work of Julia Clements and such flower-arranging gardeners as Beth Chatto.

In larger gardens the idea of the woodland area had developed and matured to include rhododendrons, magnolias and exotic trees, many of which had been introduced from Asia and South America earlier in the century. Bodnant in north Wales, Trewithen (pp. 46–49) and Sheffield Park in East Sussex are only three examples of these. On a smaller scale, Vita Sackville-West began gardening at Sissinghurst (pp. 67–69), influenced by Lawrence Johnstone at Hidcote Manor in Gloucestershire and Norah Lindsay at Sutton Courtenay (pp. 32–35).

The first gardens to open for the National Gardens Scheme were mostly large estates in the countryside. The ten gardens in this chapter – most of them owned by the same family for generations – are typical of those. All except one of these had a history of gardening before the beginning of the twentieth century; none was in a town. In several cases succeeding generations had swept away the earlier gardens, but Melbourne Hall (pp. 26–31) has remained close to its original design for 300 years. Hestercombe (pp. 60–65) is unusual in that there are three gardens of different eras side by side. In others – Blickling Hall and Welbeck Abbey (pp. 36–39 and 58–59) – the original landscape design remained as a framework for later changes. Landscape gardens at Erddig (pp. 40–41) and Panshanger (above) survived into the twentieth century, but Erddig deteriorated after the Second World War and was rescued by the National Trust; Panshanger was sold and the house

A view of the lake and house at Panshanger Park in Hertfordshire, from 1936. The site of the house was chosen by Humphry Repton in the early nineteenth century for its view of the river valley, which he enlarged to make the lake. The garden was opened for the National Gardens Scheme in 1927, but after the war the house was demolished, although much of the Reptonian landscape survives.

demolished in the 1950s. An important spur to gardening in Victorian and Edwardian times was the introduction of new plants, which led to the rise of both the skilled head gardener, required to produce flowers, fruit and vegetables for his employers, and a 'new class of gardeners who are more interested in plants than plans', and who created the woodland gardens. Of the former, Welbeck Abbey, Arley Hall (pp. 54–57) and Newby Hall (pp. 42–45) are examples; Trewithen and Ramster (above and pp. 50–53) are the woodland gardens. The last of the ten is the Manor House, Sutton Courtenay, the owner of which was an important influence on the gardens at Hidcote and Sissinghurst – in both cases in what has come to be called the cottage-garden style.

Garden visiting in the 1920s was not the habit that it is now, and at this distance in time it is difficult to imagine what persuaded the owners to open their gardens in 1927. There were links between several of them: the Duchess of Portland (Welbeck Abbey) and Norah Lindsay (Manor House, Sutton Courtenay) moved in the same social circles, especially early in the century. Norah Lindsay's sister and some of her gardening friends and clients were also among those who opened their gates for the scheme in the early years.

After the Second World War, when the National Trust began to take on gardens and garden visiting grew, most of those in this group began to open more frequently, but maintained their support of the NGS. But they have also had to change from being primarily for private enjoyment to providing public entertainment. More visitors meant more wear and tear, as well as requiring long-term seasonal interest. The days have gone when a herbaceous border was planted to be at its height when the owners were in residence, when rose gardens were all Hybrid Teas, and when iris borders were planted to be seen in early summer.

In 1927 Melbourne Hall in Derbyshire was owned by Captain Philip Kerr, whose family had lived there since the early seventeenth century. The garden was then and is now considered to be the best surviving example of a post-Restoration landscape in England – an English interpretation of the French style of André Le Notre at the Palace of Versailles.

The maker of the garden was Thomas Coke, a member of parliament and vice-chamberlain to Queen Anne's household. He had spent some of his early life in The Netherlands, with a tutor in Rotterdam, and inherited the estate in 1696 when in his early twenties. During the following two

Right
The east front of the
house, as seen from the
terraced lawns in 1928.

Right, bottom
The magnificent Four Seasons
Vase is sited in the Crow Walk,
the main avenue in the
wooded landscape to the
south of Melbourne Hall. The
lead vase was made by John
van Nost, who made many
other statues that are still in
the garden.

Overleaf
In recent years
more flower borders
have been introduced. This
is the Bog Garden, with
candelabra primulas,
meconopsis and corydalis
planted beside the stream.

summers, he returned to The Netherlands, and one can suppose that he visited the splendid baroque garden of Het Loo Palace, which was then being expanded. He made plans for his new garden and consulted the owners of the best-known nursery of the time: George London, who had worked at Versailles, and Henry Wise of Brompton Park Nurseries. They gave him advice on the proposed garden, and supplied him with quantities of plants.

The house stands on a slight rise, from where grassed terraces run down to the Great Basin, which was formed from fish ponds. On the far side of the basin is a wrought-iron arbour, the best-known feature of the garden, made on site by a skilled blacksmith, Robert Bakewell, about 1705. It is generally known as the Birdcage.

On the south side of the garden is the Grove, where Coke planted avenues of lime and hornbeam and made a pattern of walks and vistas, each ending in a carefully sited fountain, statue or vase. The most famous of these is the Four Seasons Vase, of lead, which was made by John van Nost, a Flemish sculptor who worked in England. It is believed to have been given to Coke by Queen Anne.

By 1725 the garden was deemed to be finished. But gardens become overgrown, and at about the

The NGS gardens I hugely admire share certain characteristics that I think are crucial: appropriateness to location, coherent design, interesting plants and really high standards of horticulture. Also energy, atmosphere, birdsong and the personal involvement of their owners.

Kathryn Bradley-Hole, Gardens Editor of *Country Life*

time of the First World War, into the 1920s, a great many laurels planted by the Victorian members of the family were removed as they were obscuring the design of the garden.

The garden opened for the NGS in 1927 and continued to do so regularly for more than thirty years. Since the early 1990s, with the gardens open several days a week from April to September, there has been more planting in the informal parts of the garden to extend the season of interest. Candelabra primulas, meconopsis and irises grow along the banks of the stream, rhododendrons and magnolias are in flower in spring, roses and herbaceous borders continue the display and an arboretum has been planted. Trees that had grown too tall were removed before they obscured the view from the house to the Birdcage, and the wood behind the Birdcage has been cleared, extending the view to the fields beyond. But the garden remains as an English interpretation of a continental garden fashion.

The Top Border at Melbourne Hall, with its buttresses of yew, is planted with bearded iris, nepeta, geranium and variegated pittosporum.

More planting in the Bog Garden, with irises, candelabra primulas and a large-leaved rhubarb relative. A wisteria gives height in the background.

The shrubby growth that formed a background to the Birdcage has been cleared away to give a long view over the fields beyond.

The Birdcage, a famous feature in the garden, dates from 1705. Thomas Coke chose a wrought-iron version of the more usual temple in contemporary gardens.

The very English garden at the Manor House in Sutton Courtenay, Oxfordshire, is known for its creator, Norah Lindsay. She started gardening twelve years before Lawrence Johnstone at Hidcote and thirty-five years before Vita Sackville-West at Sissinghurst, but she was a friend of both, and her garden style had a considerable influence on their respective gardens.

Norah Lindsay was married in 1895, and the house and surroundings were a wedding present to her husband, Harry. The couple started to improve their new home, he in the house and she in the garden. She had no training in gardening, and did not use a professional designer, but she did have a natural artistic bent. She read Gertrude Jekyll's books, many of which were published in the first years of the century, and the new magazines, such as *Country Life* and *House and Garden*. When the Lindsays went on holiday to Italy and France, Norah visited gardens and made notes on their design.

Ten years after she had begun gardening, an illustrated article about the Manor House appeared in *Country Life*, describing the garden in three parts: the Long Garden and parallel Persian Garden, the Pleasaunce or Wilderness, and the River Garden. Norah's gardening was *laissez-faire*; she allowed plants room to grow so that there was an impression of abundance; there was to be no bare earth, and she was pleased when her plants seeded themselves in unexpected places. She was careful in her use of colour and always planted so as to provide interest throughout the year.

During the First World War, when her husband was away in the army, Norah continued to garden, but sacrificed some of her flower borders to grow vegetables. After the war, she and Harry separated. Norah stayed at Sutton Courtenay, but found it hard to pay for the upkeep of the house. The answer to her financial problems was to use her gift for garden design to help her many friends with their gardens, on a professional basis.

The wisteria-clad wall and gateway at the side of Sutton Courtenay Manor House. In the background are the tops of the gateposts of the former entrance to the house.

Daffodils were planted on the banks of the stream that runs through the garden at Sutton Courtenay, and which eventually joins the River Thames.

The Long Garden in about 1931, with Norah Lindsay's exuberant planting in borders edged with clipped box, and Irish upright yews to bring a sense of Italy into the garden.

Colonel Harry Lindsay and Norah pictured at the entrance to the Manor House in 1907. There is a new entrance today, but the gateposts remain, incorporated into the garden (see photograph opposite).

The Manor House opened for the NGS for one day in 1927, but did not open again until the late 1930s, perhaps because Norah was busy with her clients. In 1931 she wrote an article about her garden for *Country Life*. It includes many of her ideas on gardening: choosing plants to ensure a succession of flowering; keeping pale and strong flower colours apart; combining silvery plants with the golds of rudbeckias and the yellows of sunflowers; using fastigiate conifers for emphasis; adding seats and focal points; and using roses everywhere. She was an enthusiast for all roses.

Norah made a success of her garden-design business, but when the Second World War was declared the Manor House was shut up and she went to stay with friends and family. Later in the war the house was requisitioned for use as a girls' school, and Norah did not return. It was sold in 1945 and she died in 1948.

The buyer was David Astor, who would go on to edit *The Observer* newspaper for twenty-seven

years, who had stayed at Sutton Courtenay before the war, when he had helped Norah in the garden. Once the sale had been completed, he asked Brenda Colvin, a founder member of the Institute of Landscape Architects, to advise on alterations following the years of neglect. Much of Norah's flower-filled garden had disappeared: the Long Garden was 'an empty expanse', but was left as a lawn with a herbaceous border against the wall; the Persian Garden, where Norah Lindsay had grown many of her roses, became a parterre with lavender, roses and lilies; and the river walks were developed with bulbs in the grass and more tree-planting.

David Astor died in 2001, and the house has new owners. Today, it is hard to imagine the 1930s garden. Some of the Lindsay upright yews in the Long Garden, the vine pergola and the hornbeam *allée* remain. Brenda Colvin's parterre in the Jewel Garden and the paved terrace in front of the house are still features. A few of Norah Lindsay's roses are still growing in the garden, and the present owners are planting more of her favourites. Their aim is to bring back some of her flower-filled garden, and to maintain Brenda Colvin's vistas.

The Long Garden as it is today. Some of Norah Lindsay's Irish yews remain.

Norah Lindsay had an influence on another large garden, that of Blickling Hall in Aylsham, Norfolk. Little is known about the first garden on the site, which was laid out by the builder of the house, Sir Henry Hobart, and was swept away in the early eighteenth century by the next owner, the 1st Earl of Buckingham. His garden included a new woodland with formal paths, a pond and a parterre. By the 1760s such formalism was out, and the second earl introduced wandering paths in the woodlands and planted informal groups of trees. Various statues, columns and a fountain were brought into the garden from local house sales, and an orangery, probably designed by Samuel Wyatt, was built in 1780.

When Lord Buckingham died in 1793, Blickling Hall passed to his second daughter, Lady Suffield, who lived there until her death in 1850 at the age of eighty-three. A gardener herself, she employed John Adey Repton, the eldest son

Top
The impressive approach
to Blickling Hall.

Above
The formal garden
in 1910, as designed by
Lady Lothian.

Opposite, top
The formal garden as it is
today. Norah Lindsay's
simplification of the elaborate
parterre (see p. 39) is
maintained with planting in her
style and the acorn-shaped
topiary she introduced.

Opposite, bottom
In late summer, the borders
contain nasturtiums, yellow
solidago and erigeron.

of Humphry Repton, to help her with her flower garden, as well as to design improvements to the house. Some of his sketches for the ornamentation of her garden survive.

The next change to the gardens came in the 1860s, when the eighth Marquess of Lothian was living there. He made great changes to both the house and the garden, which was said to be a wilderness at that time. Formality was back in fashion, and plans were made for a new parterre in front of the east side of the house. The son of W.A. Nesfield (a notable constructor of Victorian parterres) was consulted about the considerable amount of earth-moving needed. But the design of the parterre was by Lady Lothian, who placed a fountain at its centre. From the terrace above the parterre there was a view of the borders and beyond to the temple and the park. Conifers and shrubs were planted on each side of the vista.

After Lady Lothian died, in 1901, Blickling Hall was let for several years. It was one of the tenants, Mrs C.H. Hoffman, who opened the gardens for three days in 1927 for the NGS. The gardens opened regularly for the scheme until

I still feel a pang in the middle of June as I remember when our house in the Cotswolds was open to the public – a band playing on the lawn, teas being served from a barn, the garden a riot of reds and pinks, and the scent of roses hanging in the air. We've since sold the house, but I'm still an avid follower of the NGS. It is a wonderful opportunity to spend the day with fellow garden lovers, gathering ideas and sharing experiences.

Anneka Rice, television presenter

Herbaceous planting against the south wall of the parterre: alchemilla, lythrum, campanula and astilbe.

The border on the terrace at the front of the house, overlooking the parterre, has a red–orange–yellow theme, with dahlia, helenium, crocosmia, achillea and fennel.

The dry moat, also planted by Norah Lindsay, contains ferns, Japanese anemones and hostas, with a wisteria over the archway.

1940, the responsibility for opening being taken over in 1932 by the eleventh Marquess of Lothian, who, after inheriting the estate, had decided to live there. He modernized the house and called in Norah Lindsay to help with the garden. The Victorian parterre had already been criticized for being over-elaborate and labour-intensive, and Norah simplified the planting, making four beds of colourful herbaceous plants, with an acorn-shaped clipped yew at the corners of each bed. Surrounding these beds were L-shaped beds of roses and nepeta. Norah left in place the so-called 'grand pianos' of clipped yew just beyond the parterre.

Norah also introduced flowering shrubs to the planting on either side of the Temple Walk, replacing a line of conifers with 600 azaleas and rhododendrons. She planted magnolias in the dry moat that abuts three sides of the house, and hydrangeas in the Terrace Garden. In the Wilderness she planted thousands of bulbs in the grass along the avenues, which now make a colourful display in spring.

In 1940, with the death of the Marquess, the estate was bequeathed to the National Trust. During the war it was requisitioned for use as the officers' mess for the nearby airfield, and when de-requisitioned it was again let for several years. In 1960 the Trust started work to restore the house and gardens, and it was opened to the public in 1962.

There have recently been more developments in the garden, and a double border of herbaceous perennials, shrubs and grasses has been planted on the terrace above the parterre, which remains as Norah Lindsay designed it. In the Wilderness, north of the Temple Walk, is the Secret Garden, formerly Lady Suffield's flower garden, with a summer house, scented plants and one of John Repton's seats. Near by, close to the orangery, there is a new garden of camellias and other shade-loving plants. In the orangery itself is a collection of many kinds of citrus plant.

The border on the terrace at the front of the house, overlooking the parterre, has a red–orange–yellow theme, with dahlia, helenium, crocosmia, achillea and fennel.

The dry moat, also planted by Norah Lindsay, contains ferns, Japanese anemones and hostas, with a wisteria over the archway.

The garden at Erddig Hall near Wrexham in north Wales is part of an estate that has belonged to the Yorke family for almost 300 years. The first Yorke, Simon, inherited the estate in 1733 from his uncle, who had extended the garden from the original walled plot, to include a canal, a bowling green and a vegetable garden, and planted more fruit trees on the walls. Simon continued his uncle's tree-planting, but his son, Philip, had grander ideas, commissioning William Emes (a contemporary of Lancelot 'Capability' Brown), who worked chiefly in the Midlands (see Arley Hall, pp. 54–57) and Wales, to make plans for 'improving' the park. Emes worked at Erddig for thirteen years, building an ice house, adding to the walks in the pleasure ground, making terraces and constructing the unusual weir, known as the Cup and Saucer, to control the regular flooding of the local river.

Philip Yorke died in 1804, and there were no major changes in the garden until about the middle of the century, when box-enclosed borders were added to the parterre in front of the house — a Victorian fashion. The water supply to the house was improved by the installation of a ram pump, and this enabled two fountains to be set in the parterre as part of the design. Many more trees were planted, including an ornamental avenue featuring some recently introduced species (wellingtonia, monkey puzzle, Douglas fir and cedars); towards the end of the century rhododendrons and other flowering shrubs were introduced.

The shortage of labour after the First World War meant that it was impossible to keep the garden in good condition, although it opened for the NGS in 1927. In the NGS archive is a letter from Mrs Yorke, who wrote before the opening that the trees were a special feature, that July and August were the best months for opening and that she did not want the opening to be an annual affair. Nevertheless, Erddig did continue to open annually in July or August. After the Second World War there were no gardeners, and little was done on the estate. The owner used sheep as his lawnmowers, which kept down the seedling trees but did not control the weeds. There was some subsidence in both house and garden because of coalmining near by.

In 1973 the property was given to the National Trust, which initiated a thorough restoration of both house and garden and opened the estate to the public in 1977. The canal was cleaned out, overgrown beech trees were cut down and the shapeless Irish yews in the yew walk were pruned hard and fed, and recovered. Old apple cultivars were planted as orchard blocks, and old daffodil cultivars planted at their feet. Many cultivars of pear and stone fruit were known to have been grown at Erddig in the eighteenth century, and as many as could be obtained were trained against the walls, with some nineteenth-century daffodil cultivars planted around them. On another of the garden walls on the south side of the garden is a National Collection of ivy (*Hedera*), which contains nine species and eighty-five cultivars. Also of interest in winter is a collection of holly (*Ilex*) that replaces earlier variegated hollies. Planting in the Victorian parterre by the house is seasonal but colourful, and a garden of roses and clematis reflects what is known of the Victorian original.

There are also National Collections at Newby Hall, near Ripon in North Yorkshire, and Trewithen, near Truro in Cornwall. Newby was built at the end of the 1600s by Sir Edward Blackett MP, whose gardener was Peter Aram. Aram had been apprenticed to George London and Henry Wise, owners of Brompton Park Nurseries and designers of the garden at Hampton Court, south-west of the capital. Aram's design for Newby, probably created with the advice of London, consisted of avenues of lime trees and square grass plots ornamented by statues. There is still an avenue of limes in the garden.

In the mid-eighteenth century the house was sold to William Weddell, also an MP, who altered and enlarged the house and landscaped its immediate surroundings. Weddell's heirs made few changes to the garden, although a rock garden was built in the late nineteenth century by Backhouse Nurseries of York, and still survives.

The estate was inherited in 1921 by Major Edward Compton, who took his time starting the planting of the garden while a shelter belt grew up. The house was surrounded by Victorian parterres, with elaborate planting schemes; these he removed and replaced with a lily pond on the south side. Realizing that the view from the house to the River Ure should be the main axis of the garden, he planted the vista with a double herbaceous border backed by solid yew hedges. On each side of this feature, one is led to smaller, compartmentalized gardens that are of interest during different seasons. One of the first to be made was Sylvia's Garden, named for Compton's wife and planted for spring interest. The garden at Hidcote Manor in Gloucestershire had been started just before that at Newby Hall, and it is suggested that Compton may have been influenced by it, for instance when laying out the enclosed gardens.

Two views of the herbaceous borders at Newby Hall in the late 1930s.

The south front of
Newby Hall is seen from the
river end of the herbaceous
borders. To the right and left
are more compartmentalized
gardens, such as the Rose
Garden, the Water Garden
and the Autumn Garden.

The opposite view,
from the house to the River
Ure, shows the formal pond
in the foreground.

The garden at Newby opened for the NGS for the first time in September 1929, and has continued to open regularly. Compton made more changes in the 1930s, replacing a tennis court with a garden of old-fashioned roses, and a croquet lawn with an autumn garden. Other plantings in the 1930s were *Acer griseum*, the paperbark maple, one of which is now the county champion for girth and height, and *Laburnum × watereri* 'Vossii', which has hanging racemes of flower, along the approach to the Rock Garden. The latter may be the first example of a laburnum tunnel, a feature made famous by those in the gardens at Bodnant and at Barnsley House in Gloucestershire.

In 1977 Edward Compton died and was succeeded by his son Robin. After fifty or more years, parts of the garden were over-mature; it was also proving labour-intensive. Some of the trees needed to be thinned out, and a lot of replanting was required. Among the new plants introduced was the genus *Cornus*, and this has flourished in the conditions. There are now forty-two species

and sixty-two cultivars dispersed around the garden, and they have been designated a National Collection by the charity Plant Heritage.

The Rose Garden, which had included a collection of old-fashioned roses, was in need of rejuvenation. New plants were brought in, and in the garden today are beds of all groups, albas, noisettes, gallicas, centifolias and more. In the centre is a circular pool with a fountain. On the other side of the herbaceous border is the Autumn Garden, which has a similar pool and fountain at its centre. Here are planted such late-flowering perennials as dahlias and salvias with shrubs, including hydrangeas.

Newby Hall has developed enormously since it first opened for the NGS, and has won several awards. It is now in the care of the third generation of Comptons, who continue to bring in new plants and ideas while retaining the basic design. It is open regularly on its own terms in the garden season, with a steam railway, restaurant and garden centre, but still supports the NGS as well.

Above
The Rose Garden at Newby Hall, planted with old-fashioned shrub species and varieties, has a central fountain and pool.

Opposite
In the Autumn Garden, dahlias, crocosmia, salvia, hydrangea and sedum are planted for late-season colour. The urn-fountain in the centre mirrors that of the Rose Garden on the opposite side of the herbaceous border.

The house, garden and parkland of Trewithen, meanwhile, have been in the same family since the early eighteenth century, and an early owner was an enthusiastic planter of trees. The Cornish name Trewithen means 'house in the spinney', and by the time George Johnstone inherited the estate in 1904 the house was surrounded by trees. Johnstone's first action was to thin them out, leaving some for shelter, since the garden is only a few miles from the sea. One of his early plantings was 100 specimens of *Rhododendron arboreum*, and of those that remain, one has been measured as the tallest in the British Isles.

Johnstone also removed the trees facing the south front of the house, leaving a clear grassed space about 120 yards (110 m) long, and began planting trees and shrubs on each side. This was at a time when many new plants were being introduced from Asia, and this area has now matured into a renowned collection. The Cornish

Trewithen is not only camellias and rhododendrons: the walled garden is Edwardian in feel, with formal box-edged beds and standard roses, and a pergola.

climate has allowed many of the less hardy plants to flourish outside.

Johnstone was a friend of J.C. Williams of Caerhays Castle, another great Cornish garden, to the south of St Austell. The Williams family had sponsored the expeditions of several plant-collectors in the late nineteenth and early twentieth centuries, among them E.H. Wilson, George Forrest and Frank Kingdon-Ward, and as part of their sponsorship received many of the seeds brought back by the travellers. Some also came to Johnstone, and many of the magnolias at Trewithen grew from wild-collected seeds. Magnolias grow well there, and Johnstone became an authority on their botany and culture; his book *Asiatic Magnolias in Cultivation* was published by the RHS in 1955.

Camellias are also an important genus in the garden, and it is a good home for some of the more tender ones. A hardy camellia, now widely grown in many gardens, is *Camellia* × *williamsii* 'Donation', which was named after the owner of Caerhays. He had sent seeds from a Forrest expedition to Colonel Stephenson Clarke of Borde Hill in Sussex, who raised hybrid plants that he named *Camellia* × *williamsii*. He gave two plants to Williams and kept one for himself; Williams gave one to Johnstone. Both the Stephenson Clarke and the Williams plants died, so all the plants now grown have come from the Trewithen plant. The camellia collection is exceptional, and in 2012 Trewithen was cited as an International Camellia Garden of Excellence, reflecting the variety and quality of the camellias grown.

But there are many other rare plants in the garden, as well as those of Asian origin, for expeditions to South America were also supported. Among those introductions are embothriums, myrtles and eucryphias, two of the last being champion trees of the British Isles for girth.

The south lawn is bordered by trees and shrubs, including rhododendrons, magnolias and azaleas.

The recently planted rose garden includes about 3000 plants in borders that form a Celtic cross.

George Johnstone raised several new plants of his own breeding. *Rhododendron* 'Trewithen Orange' won the RHS Reginald Cory Cup for the best new hybrid of the year in 1955. *Camellia reticulata* 'Trewithen Pink' also won an award from the RHS. *Ceanothus arboreus* 'Trewithen Blue' is available from nurseries, and Johnstone named many daffodils of his own raising, among them 'Green Howard', 'Winter' and 'Trewithen'.

The present members of the family are still developing the garden. A rose garden was planted in 2008, with the aim of showing that roses could be grown successfully in Cornwall, and all kinds of rose are now flourishing in an open, southwest-facing area. Ferns are being planted in the quarry (which, it is thought, was a cock-fighting pit in the eighteenth century), where alpine rhododendrons, meconopsis and primulas are already established.

The woodland garden at Ramster near Haslemere, Surrey, was started by the business-man Sir Harry Waechter, who bought the property in 1890. He converted the existing farmhouse into an Edwardian mansion and bought some neighbouring fields. The land was oak woodland, and the trees an ideal canopy for rhododendrons. When planting his garden, Sir Harry sought the help of a nearby nursery, Gauntlett & Co., which specialized in bamboos, tree peonies, 'Himalayan Rhododendrons and Japanese Maples', imported from Japan. It supplied the ornaments, such as stone lanterns and cranes, that can still be seen in the garden. Many of the plants are still in the garden, notably the avenue of *Acer palmatum* var. *dissectum* planted as twenty-year-old trees in the early twentieth century.

In 1922 the property was bought by Sir Henry Norman, a journalist, member of parliament and cabinet minister who was married to a daughter of the first Lord Aberconway, owner of Bodnant garden. Lady Norman, who had been brought up at Bodnant, was an enthusiastic gardener and continued to develop the garden at Ramster. She planted more rhododendrons and azaleas (Exbury and Mollis types), as well as magnolias and camellias and other flowering plants that flourished in the acid soil. Rhododendrons were a special interest, and she raised many plants from seeds brought back from Asia by such collectors as George Forrest. She also did some plant-breeding of her own, raising many hybrids. Some of these are still in the garden, but most of the labels and plant records have been lost.

Ramster was among the gardens to open in the first years of the NGS, opening each May, and has continued to open regularly for the scheme for more than sixty years. An *Acer grosseri* var. *hersii* tree was presented to the garden by the NGS to commemorate this long period of fund-raising.

The garden is now looked after by Lady Norman's granddaughter, Miranda Gunn, also an

The lake at Ramster is ringed by tall rhododendrons, seen here reflected in the water. A large leaf of gunnera is in the foreground.

A cherry tree and rhododendron form a light canopy over the bluebells coming into bloom by the lake.

In May, the woodland paths are lined with rhododendrons and bluebells.

There is still a Japanese influence in the garden at Ramster, with a stone lantern by the century-old avenue of *Acer palmatum* var. *dissectum*.

Vistas are important at Ramster. The trees form an excellent canopy for the rhododendrons and azaleas.

enthusiast for rhododendrons, who took over in 1980. She has rescued some of her grandmother's hybrids and selected one of them for registration, naming it R. 'Fay Norman' in her honour. In 1999 she became involved in collecting a group of so-called Hardy Hybrid rhododendrons; these are rhododendrons raised between 1840 and 1940, most by British nurseries but some by Belgian and Dutch nurseries. They make large plants and are very tough, but are out of fashion in these days of smaller gardens. The collection at present consists of 170 varieties, but more may be added. The project has the support of the RHS Rhododendron Group.

Ramster has matured into a classic woodland garden of more than 20 acres (8 ha.), with rhododendrons, magnolias and camellias, and spring bulbs and orchids in the grass beneath. In the bog garden, *Gunnera manicata* and a tree fern thrive. A garden to celebrate the millennium was created on the south side of the house using raised beds and pergolas; formed in the shape of an 'M', it is planted with sun-loving species. Ramster is open daily in spring for the rhododendron and magnolia season, and briefly in autumn for the maple colour.

In May the rhododendrons and azaleas are in full bloom.

The maple avenue is pictured here in the 1930s.

While Ramster remains a family garden maintained by three generations, Arley Hall near Knutsford in Cheshire boasts an unbroken line that runs back for several centuries. It has been in the same family since the fifteenth century, and all generations seem to have cultivated a garden, often (but not always) the women of the house. The earliest record of a garden at Arley is a map of 1744, although little remains of that garden.

It is known that the landscape surrounding the garden was designed by William Emes (see Erddig, pp. 40–41) in the 1780s, but the basic design of the present garden round the house was by Rowland Egerton-Warburton and his wife, who built the present house between 1832 and 1845 and then started to develop the garden. It was a family garden, including a kitchen garden to produce fruit, flowers and vegetables for the house. The famous herbaceous borders were planted in about 1846 and are claimed to have started the fashion

The gateway leading from the herbaceous borders to the walled garden is edged with dividing buttresses.

In the middle of the Walled Garden is a pond with the Elizabeth Ashbrook Fountain (see pp. 56–57) at its centre.

for such borders in later Victorian and Edwardian times. Subsequent refinements were the insertion of four buttresses of yew in each side, and the grassing over of the gravel walk in the centre.

The Ilex Avenue, at right angles to the herbaceous borders, is another frequently photographed feature. Seven pairs of evergreen oaks were planted in the 1850s and initially formed pillars with rounded tops; but with the scarcity of gardeners during the First World War they were not pruned, and when brought under control again were trained as flat-topped columns. These are now 26 feet (8 m) tall and make a strong sculptural statement in the garden.

Next to the herbaceous borders is the Tea Cottage, where tea parties were held in Victorian times. There were initially formal beds of Hybrid Tea roses here, together with a topiary garden, but they were removed in 1961 and replanted with old-fashioned and shrub roses by Elizabeth, Viscountess Ashbrook, who was influenced by Vita Sackville-West's articles in *The Observer* and by the horticulturist Graham Stuart Thomas.

At the end of the Ilex Avenue is the Rootery, constructed in the 1870s as a miniature alpine landscape. In the 1930s scented azaleas were introduced, but the trees had grown up and shaded the garden so that it became unsuitable for the alpines. In 1960 it was time to rethink, putting in plants that would grow in the altered conditions. The azaleas had done well, so more were planted, with rhododendrons, Japanese maples and ferns.

Next to the Ilex Avenue there was a bowling green, set in a sunken garden, but after the First

Right, from top
The herbaceous borders in 1927, before the gravel path was replaced by grass; the rose garden and Tea Cottage in the 1930s; the Flag Garden, made in about 1900, was named after its stone paving, and was planted mainly with roses; fruit trees in the walled garden in winter.

World War part of it was remade into a tennis court (now a hard court), while the rest was laid out as a small pool surrounded by low-growing conifers and *Alchemilla*. This is the Fish Garden, made by the present owner's grandmother.

Until the Second World War, the Walled Garden was one of the kitchen gardens that supplied the house with fruit and vegetables, and which contained beds of flowers for colour or for cutting. After the war they were run as a commercial market garden for about twenty years, but when that became uneconomical, Elizabeth Ashbrook made a major change, turning one of them into a flower garden. She planted more climbers against the walls and filled the borders with a mixture of herbaceous and shrubby plants. The pond was moved to the centre, together with four Dawyck beeches (*Fagus sylvatica* 'Dawyck', the upright cultivar) to make a square. In 2006, after her death, a fountain in the form of an opening flower was placed in the centre of the

Below
The alcove at the end of the double herbaceous border in early summer. The border was first planted more than 150 years ago.

Opposite, top
At the centre of one of the former kitchen gardens is a wirework arbour, brought to Arley from Ireland.

Opposite, bottom
The Ilex Avenue of evergreen oaks was one of the original plantings in the garden.

My family and I have spent many happy afternoons visiting the wonderful gardens of Northumberland and the Borders. Favourites include Nunwick, home of the Allgood family, the Duke of Sutherland's garden at Merton and Humphry Wakefield's at Chillingham.

Chris Mullin, diarist and Labour politician

pond in her memory. Vegetables and flowers are still grown in the Kitchen Garden, which was redesigned in the 1990s by Zoe, Viscountess Ashbrook, Elizabeth's daughter-in-law. This has as its centrepiece a white arbour of delicate wirework, which came from Ireland, from the family home of the father of the present Viscount Ashbrook. The Arbour Walk is covered with climbing roses, complemented by tulips in spring and cardoons and annuals in summer.

An area known as the Grove, to the north of the house, has been woodland since the 1750s. However, it has been developed since 1970 by the present Viscount Ashbrook, and is now a maturing woodland garden. Many of the old trees were removed and beds made for rhododendrons and azaleas. Taller trees, such as magnolias, camellias, cornus (dogwood), ornamental cherries, birches and sorbus (rowan), have been planted in subsequent years, with spring bulbs in the grass below.

There are records of gardens at Welbeck Abbey near Worksop, Nottinghamshire, for the last 400 years, but details of these early gardens are rather sparse. A seventeenth-century survey shows a walled area used as a kitchen garden, with a formal canal; it was replaced in the eighteenth century by a landscape designed by Francis Richardson, and a new walled garden was made. Towards the end of that century, the new walled area was being used as a kitchen garden by the 3rd Duke of Portland's head gardener, William Speechley. Renowned for growing exotic fruits, including pineapples and grapes, Speechley also undertook considerable tree-planting on the estate, so much so that when Humphry Repton was commissioned to make improvements, he recommended some thinning of the trees. Three of Repton's 'Red Books' detail the improvements he made to the estate between 1790 and 1803. Some of his work remains: the considerable earthworks around the abbey, the extension and deepening of the lake, and walks in the grounds.

The 5th duke (1800–1879), although something of a recluse, was very active on the estate. He built a new walled kitchen garden of 22 acres (9 ha.), including greenhouses for growing out-of-season and exotic fruit. The 6th duke (1857–1943) and his wife, prominent members of Edwardian society, made more changes to the garden. A rhododendron valley, a double herbaceous border, a formal rose garden and a sunken garden with pools were all laid out in their time. The duke employed Messrs Parsons and Partridge, a landscape firm, between 1899 and 1905 to help with this construction and planting ('Parsons' was Alfred Parsons, a landscape painter and illustrator). Also among the features introduced by the duke were the pergola and two ponds, in the Duchess's Garden; the pergola and one of the ponds still survive. At the beginning of the twentieth century the gardens were renowned for

The gardens at Welbeck Abbey were in their prime in the early twentieth century. After the Second World War the estate was leased to the Ministry of Defence, and, with only minimal maintenance, the decorative borders have largely disappeared.

Left
The pergola in the Duchess's Garden, at Welbeck Abbey with roses and other climbers; it surrounds two semicircular ponds.

Left, centre top and bottom
Herbaceous borders at either side of the pergola are backed by hedges of yew and ivy. Variegated maples give height and lightness against this background.

Left, bottom
Irises and agapanthus are planted beside one of the pools.

the high standard of cultivation; a contributor to the *Gardener's Magazine* of 1910 writes about a herbaceous border almost a quarter of a mile long, an acre of asparagus, twelve vineries and more greenhouses to supply decorative plants for the house.

The First World War affected such lavishness, however, and an issue of the *Gardeners' Chronicle* of 1924 reports that the kitchen garden had been leased to the pre-war head gardener for the commercial growing of fruit and vegetables. The flower gardens remained to provide pleasant surroundings for the Portlands' guests and decoration for the house, and in 1927 the gardens were opened to raise money for the Queen Alexandra Memorial Fund, which was later transformed into the NGS. The duke was then

chairman of the fund, so was under something of an obligation to open, which he did on 6 June and 25 August. Many people were attracted on both days, at a charge of a shilling a head, and on 6 June the amount raised was £234. 17s. 6d, at the time the national record for a single day.

The abbey was leased to the Ministry of Defence from 1946 to 2005, and much of the cultivated garden from the 1930s has disappeared. The family returned to the estate in 2005, and new formal gardens have been made around the house. Borders of roses and herbaceous perennials have been established on the east terrace, a parterre and orchard have been re-established to the south of the house, and at the south-east corner of the house is a productive potager. The gardens are no longer open to the public.

The intriguing garden at Hestercombe in Cheddon Fitzpaine, Somerset, incorporates three styles: the eighteenth-century landscape garden designed by Coplestone Warre Bampfylde (1720–1791); the nineteenth-century Victorian parterre; and the formal Edwardian garden. The last was commissioned by the Hon. Edward Portman from Edwin Lutyens, with planting by Gertrude Jekyll. After the Second World War, the garden suffered from a shortage of labour, but it has now been restored and is under the care of the Hestercombe Trust.

The estate was inherited in 1750 by Bampfylde, who was a talented landscape painter and a friend of Henry Hoare of Stourhead, Wiltshire. Bampfylde created his relatively small landscape garden in the style of 'Capability' Brown between 1751 and 1786, including various buildings, such as a temple and mausoleum; a lake; and seats to contemplate the views. The garden was much admired at the time, especially the Great Cascade, which is said to have been inspired by the more famous contemporary garden the Leasowes in Shropshire, designed by William Shenstone.

Bampfylde's successors died in 1872 and the estate was bought by the 1st Viscount Portman.

Below
Bampfylde's landscape garden rises above the Pear Pond.

Bottom left
The Victorian Terrace above the Great Plat at Hestercombe, with summer bedding of cannas, lobelia, pelargoniums and salvia.

Bottom
The Mill Pond, below the Pear Pond, is the lowest of those in the landscape garden.

Opposite
The restoration work at Hestercombe has involved the thinning of the woodland.

The Great Plat in 1927
(left) and as it looks today,
following restoration.

Portman presented the estate to his grandson as a wedding gift in 1892, and in 1903 Edward Portman commissioned the young Edwin Lutyens to design a flower garden in front of the house. This was constructed in 1904–1906, and Gertrude Jekyll made planting plans and probably supplied the plants. In 1911 Edward Portman died, but his widow continued to live in the house. She, too, cherished the garden, which she opened for the NGS in 1927. An article in *Country Life* in that year praised the garden in its maturity, describing the plants as complementing the local stone used in the garden's construction – 'an impressionist painter would be proud to own such colour and lightness'.

During the Second World War, the house was requisitioned first by the British army and then by the Americans; Mrs Portman lived in four rooms, and was looked after by her maid and butler. The estate was sold in 1944 to the Crown Estate Commissioners to offset family death duties, and was finally derequisitioned in 1945. Mrs Portman died in 1951, and in 1953 Somerset County Council leased Hestercombe to the county fire brigade for use as its headquarters. It was stipulated that the garden and orchard should continue to be looked after, and this was done as far as was possible at the time. In 1962–63 the trees in the landscape garden, regarded as a forest, were cut down for timber, and the area replanted.

In the 1970s came the first attempts to restore the garden. The borders had become overgrown and the hard landscaping was falling into

disrepair, but it was recognized that this had been an important garden. Some of Jekyll's planting plans had been found 'in the potting shed', and more were found in the archives of the University of California. Work on the Lutyens/Jekyll garden continued for twenty years.

The most striking feature is Lutyens's Great Plat, a formal sunken square garden crossed diagonally by two grass paths, with characteristic Lutyens semicircular steps leading down to the garden at each corner. Within the triangles formed by the paths are borders edged with stone. On two outer sides are rills, flowing from semicircular pools and planted with irises and arums. The far side of the Plat is bounded by a 230-foot (70-m) pergola supporting climbing plants. On the house side, above the Plat, is the Victorian Terrace, created in the late nineteenth century when the house was being redesigned. From there one passes through the rotunda, which unites the Dutch Garden, planted in the Jekyll style with lambs' ears and lavender, and Orangery with the formal garden; beyond is the landscape garden.

In 1995 work to restore the landscape was begun. The Pear Pond was cleaned, the temple and mausoleum rebuilt, the woods thinned and the Great Cascade cleared. Restoration continues, and the fire brigade has now left the house, which has been offered to the Hestercombe Trust. There are plans to repair it and make the gardens a national centre for conservation studies.

Opposite
Lutyens's pergola is planted
with Jekyll favourites – roses
and other climbers – and
underplanted with lavender.

Top
A border in the Dutch Garden
today is planted with stachys,
roses and heliotrope around
an Italianate urn.

Above
Echinops and santolina,
contrasting blue and grey,
give a feeling of Gertrude
Jekyll's planting style.

1940–59
A New Era

Catherine Horwood

The Second World War touched the lives of everyone, and National Gardens Scheme owners were no exception. The charity's income dropped by more than two-thirds during the war years; many gardens were unable to open becase of their location or lack of gardening help. Those that did open were encouraged to make a feature of growing vegetables as part of the 'Dig for Victory' campaign.

When hostilities ended, a nostalgia for the peace and tranquillity of the countryside revived garden visiting, which became even more popular as car ownership grew. It did not take long for the NGS's income to return to pre-war levels. The opening of Windlesham Moor, home to the newly married Princess Elizabeth and Prince Philip, together with other royal estates, was particularly popular.

From the 1950s the NGS had a regular stand at the Chelsea Flower Show, and radio appeals were made by such popular figures as John Betjeman. With manufacturing restrictions lifted,

listings were printed on the now familiar bright-yellow paper, and by the end of the decade nearly 1200 gardens were opening for the scheme in England and Wales.

Sissinghurst, probably the most influential garden of the second half of the twentieth century, came to public notice when it first opened for the NGS in 1938. It soon became – and remains – a site of pilgrimage for serious gardeners across the world.

Vita Sackville-West and her husband, Harold Nicolson, bought Sissinghurst Castle near Cranbrook, Kent, in 1930 for the prosaic reason that their previous home, Long Barn (also in Kent), was about to be surrounded by an early battery chicken farm. Vita later wrote that Sissinghurst had had no garden at all: 'One might reasonably have hoped to inherit century-old hedges of yew; some gnarled mulberries; a cedar or two; a pleached alley; flagged walks; a mound. Instead there was nothing but weeds, rough

grass … wired chicken-runs, squalor and slovenly disorder everywhere.' The design template for the new garden, based on the famous compart-mentalized 'rooms', 'took a lot of square-ruled drawing-paper, india-rubber, control of temper, stakes, and string' (*Country Life*, 28 August 1942).

Vita and her husband brought all their experience of having created the Long Barn garden to bear on the barren Sissinghurst site, with its solitary tower and haphazard outbuildings. In 1938 Vita was asked by Mrs Christopher Hussey, her neighbour at Scotney Castle, to open Sissinghurst for the NGS. She was happy to do so, since she was a great admirer of the scheme and its fund-raising for the Queen's Institute of District Nursing.

On Sunday, 1 May 1938, the gates were opened and the first NGS visitors arrived, paying one shilling to get in. Despite Vita's snobbery (she referred to garden visitors as 'shillingses'), she wrote warmly in the *New Statesman* in 1939: 'These mild, gentle men and women who invade one's garden after putting their silver token into the bowl … are some of the people I most gladly welcome and salute. Between them and myself a particular form of courtesy survives, a gardener's courtesy, in a world where courtesy is giving place to rougher things.'

The NGS Sundays were so successful that Vita decided to open the garden regularly, leaving an honesty bowl on a table in the porch. The income it generated – although far less than on charity days – was a useful supplement to the gardeners' wages.

The now world-famous White Garden was created in the early 1950s, and visitor numbers grew. Cars jammed the approach lanes on open days, and a much-needed public lavatory was built. While Harold famously turned his back on visitors, Vita found opening 'a pleasure; even a

Top
Warm colours in the Cottage Garden are enhanced by *Arctotis* x *hybrida* 'Flame'.

Above
A show of roses at their peak in the White Garden in late June.

Right
Early days for the White Garden in 1942, planted only with roses in box-edged beds, and (bottom) the early pathway leading through the rock garden to the Priest's House.

form of flattery' ('Other People's Gardens', *Country Notes*, 1939). She was friendly towards those who showed an interest in the garden, and there are several stories of her digging up a piece of a plant for a visitor. Amateurs and experts alike came in droves. In the early days, she was a little more wary of the latter, writing to her husband in 1941: 'If you want really highbrow talk commend me to three experts talking about auriculas — Bloomsbury has nothing on it, I couldn't understand half they said.'

By the time of Vita's death, in 1962, visitor numbers had grown to about 25,000 a year. She had taken on the garden's first trained head gardeners, Pamela Schwerdt and Sibylle Kreutzberger, in 1959, and the pair stayed on as Sissinghurst was taken over by the National Trust in lieu of death duties. With openings now across the summer months, the challenge was to maintain the spirit of the garden while extending the flowering season.

For a while, Sissinghurst was a victim of its own success. Visitor numbers peaked at 200,000 a year in the 1980s, and entrance was restricted on some days. The National Trust had to juggle such popularity with the task of preserving the garden's poetic atmosphere. Some improvements would have met with Vita's approval, some perhaps not. Paths that had been concrete in her day have been replaced with York stone, but wild flowers are no longer allowed to seed themselves in the cracks. Sissinghurst remains one of the best-loved and most influential gardens in the world, and epitomizes the inspiration that visitors can take away from garden visits.

Its seclusion in the back lanes of Northamptonshire only adds to the charm and surprise of arriving at Cottesbrooke Hall. Few of the first paying visitors in 1942 would have had cars, and those who did would have found it hard to come by petrol for leisure trips. But Cottesbrooke's owners had thought of that, and early records show that a private bus was laid on from outside the Bricklayers Arms in nearby Creaton.

The hall was built in the early eighteenth century, but it was the arrival in 1937 of the Macdonald-Buchanan family that saw the greatest changes for 200 years. Catherine Macdonald-Buchanan, grandmother of the current owner, had the idea to move the drive and entrance hall to the north side of the building from their original south-facing position. They were replaced by living rooms facing south. Enthused by their changes to the internal layout of the house, the

I love visiting gardens. The entrance sets the scene and anticipation grows; views out and views in draw me through. It is inspiring, and often I come away with new ideas, new plant combinations and new uses. Even the smallest gardens bestow a sense of harmony, peace and, occasionally, fun.

Elizabeth Banks, President of the
Royal Horticultural Society and landscape designer

Macdonald-Buchanans brought in the renowned landscaper Geoffrey Jellicoe to design the sun-drenched terrace now fronting the family rooms.

While the bones of the park had been laid out in the eighteenth century, the Macdonald-Buchanans inherited the shape of the formal gardens as they had been planned in 1912 by the Scottish architect Robert Weir Schultz. He designed the long terrace borders and the sunken courtyard garden, with its pool and Arts and Crafts pergola. Statues bought from the great sale at Stowe in Buckinghamshire in 1922 were also added.

The decision to open Cottesbrooke's gardens to the public in 1942 shows the speed with which the Macdonald-Buchanans worked on their plans. It would also have been a great boost to the morale of the local people to have such a day out. Despite rationing, tea was available and parties were offered a tour of the glasshouses and kitchen garden.

In the 1940s, Dame Sylvia Crowe came to Cottesbrooke to rework an earlier rose garden into a pool garden with a summer house. The pool-garden planting has now been changed, although Crowe's original magnolias remain, since they are felt to be the 'throbbing heart of that garden' (in the words of the present head gardener, Phylip Statner).

As were his grandparents and father, John, before him, the current owner, Alastair Macdonald-Buchanan, is a passionate plantsman. He and Phylip Statner relish the challenge of maintaining interest for visitors now that their charity openings stretch from May to October. As is the case with many large estates, new plans have to take maintenance into account, and some areas reflect this with more relaxed planting and grass being allowed to grow through the summer.

But the desire for design-led innovation is very much alive at Cottesbrooke. The award-winning designer Arne Maynard has replanted the

Above
Large tubs of blue agapanthus
and annuals are a touch
of colour among the tightly
clipped yew cones.

Opposite
Away from the formal areas,
bulbs multiply happily on grassy
banks in the Wild Garden,
amid carpets of primroses.

north front with low, chunky beech hedges, a modern motif but also one that sits perfectly with the hall's eighteenth-century facade.

The gardens that surround the house are 'rooms' that derive their personalities from their designers. Another local and long-standing friend of Cottesbrooke is the designer James Alexander-Sinclair, who was called in to rethink the Schultz borders. As he explains: 'When I first met the borders at Cottesbrooke they were magnificent, in a slightly stiff, Grand Duchessy way. After chipping away at them for a year or so we finally made the decision to start again – leaving the architecture of the yew buttresses intact and one solitary *Rosa moyesii* 'Geranium'. The idea was to create double borders that were traditional but much more flowing and romantic than their predecessors: there are Mexican waves of herbaceous plants, streamers of annuals and splashes of tulip.' He sums up the essence of Cottesbrooke today as 'a work of cooperation', and believes that, as such, it is in a 'constant state of dynamic change'.

For more than sixty years the garden at Bramdean House in Hampshire has been very much a woman's garden. With her husband away in the army, Mrs Cecil Feilden found the property in 1944 and made the decision to buy the house. It was a wise choice. Bramdean, a charming mid-eighteenth-century building of mellow Hampshire brick, is the perfect foil for the garden that Olivia Feilden immediately started to make. Within five years, the formal overgrown framework of the garden was re-established and the walled garden planned.

While Cecil Feilden was happy to build bonfires and plant trees, it was his wife who filled the surrounding borders with old roses, clematis, shrubs and herbaceous plants. It was she who would rush out on chilly evenings when frost threatened, to cover a precious acer with sheets of *The Times*. Her only help in those early days came from a local cowman-turned-gardener, Harold Sivier, who in turn was helped by his wife on summer afternoons. He stayed for thirty-eight years until – inconveniently, according to the family – he decided to retire at the age of seventy-six.

The gates opened to the public through the NGS for the first time in 1947, with Mrs Cousins from the village sitting at the gate to take the money, as she would do for the next nineteen years. Olivia's enthusiasm for the NGS and for sharing the garden with visitors resulted in her becoming the scheme's County Organizer for Hampshire.

The garden framework she inherited was beautifully in keeping with the house, sloping away to present a long vista through the walled garden and two eighteenth-century wrought-iron gates, leading the eye up to a gazebo and clock tower. This creates three distinct areas of the garden.

Since Olivia's sudden death in 1975, the development of the garden has been carried on by her daughter, Victoria Wakefield. Victoria's devotion to the garden is not surprising, given

Opposite

At Bramdean, plants are meticulously staked and supported early each spring (top). By midsummer (centre), there is a blend of shapes and colours, while high summer (bottom) brings an explosion of colour and height.

Right

Views from the 1960s of the pool and herbaceous borders to the north of the house (top) and of the house itself from the east side of the garden (centre). The strong symmetry of the garden has always been enhanced by the magnificent gates (bottom).

that she remembers going botanizing with her grandmother as a small child, clutching a copy of Bentham and Hooker's *Wild Flowers* from 1890.

Because the back of the house faces north, there are areas that get little sun, but the clever planting of viburnums, skimmias and hydrangeas makes it an enviable spot. Along the more sheltered walls, such introductions as × *Sino-calycalycanthus raulstonii* 'Hartlage Wine', a shrub with faded maroon magnolia-like flowers, flourish. This is a perfect shrub, believes Victoria, and should be more widely grown.

Always horticulturally ambitious, Victoria took her mother's designs a step further and replanted the long herbaceous borders in the first section of the garden as mirror images of each other, probably the only matched borders on show in Britain. Every year the borders are marked out with canes in metre squares to check the accuracy of the planting, and adjustments are made.

Through the gates is the walled garden, where forty varieties of old-fashioned sweet pea are grown along with immaculate vegetables, peonies for cutting and a collection of hardy and tender nerines, which are a particular passion for Victoria.

The final area of the garden is the most natural, with striped hedges of yew and box bracketing the pathway leading up to the brick gazebo, where one turns to enjoy the long view back to the house. Grass paths snake back to the

lower lawns, which are studded with such jewels as the unusual pale-yellow-flowered *Magnolia* 'Daphne', *M.* 'Porcelain Dove', *M.* × *loebneri* 'Pirouette' and *M. stellata* 'Jane Platt'. Magnolias are not usually recommended for chalk soil, as there is at Bramdean, but all these varieties are flourishing.

The greatest change since her mother first worked on the garden, Victoria feels, is in the wider availability and choice of plants. Having been on the Herbaceous Plant and Trials committees of the Royal Horticultural Society (RHS) for many years, she has been perfectly placed to watch the fashions in perennial plants change. However, she has not been tempted by the vogue for grasses. 'I prefer to admire grasses in other settings', she says. '[Bramdean] is an old-fashioned garden, and all the better for it.'

Bramdean's famous matching herbaceous borders are seen here in a long view, with a vista through the vegetable garden towards the apple store.

Exbury, in the New Forest, Hampshire, is one of a handful of British gardens that need no introduction. It was developed and planted by Lionel de Rothschild in just over twenty years, and shortly after his death in 1942, *Country Life* praised his legacy as unsurpassed. 'Everything that is noteworthy in the world of ornamental hardy trees and shrubs … has been brought together within the confines of Exbury … it provides the fitting epitaph *Si monumentum requiris, circumspice* [If you seek a monument, look around you]' (vol. 91, p. 299).

Rothschild was always keen to become what he saw as the 'Gertrude Jekyll of the woodland garden'. Jekyll's methods with herbaceous borders, he believed, could just as easily be

Below, left
Photographs of Exbury from the 1960s show the early days of the Yardley Wood cascades (top) and the Rock Garden before the major replanting.

Below
A misty late April morning in the Azalea Bowl.

Opposite, top
An exuberant display of rhododendrons lights up the Home Wood in May.

Opposite, bottom
Varied planting of herbaceous species and grasses extends the seasons of interest through summer and beyond.

followed on a larger scale, with shrubs. The real art of gardening, he felt, was not only to group plants but also to see that colours mingled well.

By the time his son Edmund opened Exbury to the public for the NGS in 1948, it was already a renowned garden with one of the greatest collections of rhododendrons, azaleas and camellias in the world. However, despite the handsome financial support available from the Rothschild banking business – Lionel famously called himself 'a banker by hobby, a gardener by profession' – the story of the estate during the twentieth century is not without its drama.

With the outbreak of the Second World War, Lionel offered Exbury as a home for evacuees, but the navy requisitioned it with orders that it had to be cleared of all its contents in forty-eight hours. The house became a stone frigate, and one of the main bases for the planning of the Allied invasion of France. Only the formal gardens were off limits to the naval staff working there.

All the estate's gardeners had been called up, and after Lionel's death work on the gardens ground to a halt. Lionel's wife, Marie-Louise (known as 'Didi') – who had shown little interest in horticulture – stepped in and, with four staff pensioners, maintained the core of the planting with continuous weeding and tidying. She learned all the plant names, almost single-handedly preserving the knowledge of the garden for the next generation.

When Edmund returned from active service, he was filled with the same passion for Exbury as his father had felt. (They are a rare example of a father and son who were both awarded the RHS's Victoria Medal, its highest honour.) Despite his mother's work, there was still much for Edmund to do in order to revive the gardens.

The NGS open days helped to boost local morale, as everyone in post-war Britain struggled to return their lives to normal. It was not until 1955 that Edmund decided to open regularly

I am passionate about gardening. The NGS is a wonderful way of sharing the joy with fellow gardeners while raising money for charity.

Mary Berry, food writer and television presenter

Mixed tree-planting, including such smaller species as Japanese maples, in the garden's wilder areas provides spectacular colour in autumn.

to the public, and he did so on the Whitsun bank holiday. So many people came that their cars stretched all the way across the New Forest from Exbury to Beaulieu. There was no car park in those days, and so visitors had to park all over the lawns (this has since been remedied, of course).

The worst crisis to face the gardens was the great storm of 1987. 'It was a night of sheer horror', remembers Marie-Louise's grandson Nicholas. 'The swirling maelstrom literally twisted trees out of the ground … 700 major trees fell throughout the gardens in a night of carnage that brought tears to the eyes … it was heart-breaking to see such mighty leviathans reduced to matchwood.'

What kept Edmund focused was the determination that the garden should be ready to open again to the public the following spring. The clear-up started immediately, and within three months every uprooted tree had been removed. Within two or three years there was no sign of the catastrophe, and the removal of the canopy even significantly improved the flowering of many rhododendrons and azaleas. The estate is now looked after by just eight gardeners, far fewer than in Lionel's time. Mechanization helps, but even today the magnificent shrubs are still assiduously deadheaded by hand.

John Spedan Lewis is celebrated for his far-sighted philanthropic gesture of turning over his family retailing business, John Lewis department stores, to a trust, giving all his employees a share in the eponymous company as 'partners'. Less well known is his other passion – for his garden, Longstock Water Garden near Stockbridge, Hampshire. He was just as obsessive with the garden as he was with his main business interests; and it has been described (by the head gardener, Robert Ballard) as 'one man's vision of paradise'.

In 1929 Spedan Lewis bought the Leckford estate, on the edge of one of Hampshire's most beautiful rivers, the Test. By 1946 he was able to extend the estate to include Longstock House, which had previously been gardened by the Beddington family. There he set about creating an astounding water garden on the 7-acre (2.8-ha.) site. Approached artfully through a narrow entrance, the water garden and the 2½ acres (1 ha.)

Left
Longstock's astilbes relish having their feet in water.

Below
Rodgersias bow over the still waters of the lakes.

of lakes are laid out before the visitor, meandering through the emerald-green lawns and crossed by a series of bridges and causeways.

From the first, the amount of time and money involved was staggering. The ground was water-logged, and so all the initial digging had to be done by hand; it took ten years. Spedan Lewis spent every free moment overseeing the work. Still standing is the summer house, where he dealt with business from the phone line he had had specially installed, while also consulting with his gardeners and the botanist Terry Jones, who advised on suitable plant varieties for this exceptional site.

Planting plans from the early days of the garden were accompanied by breathtaking lists of plant purchases, all signed off in Spedan Lewis's characteristic green ink (green is still the company colour of the John Lewis Partnership). A bulb order from 1950 shows that 8000 daffodils were bought for £260, a sum that could have bought a small terraced house at the time.

Spedan Lewis started opening the garden just two years after having bought the estate. Central to the garden's plant collection are the true aquatics: more than forty different types of water lily, including some of the rarest examples in the world. These are surrounded by the marginal aquatics, which are happy to grow in water: not only bullrushes and kingcups but also a dazzling display of candelabra primulas flowering from March to July, followed by irises in May and then an abundance of rodgersias and astilbes.

Stepping back from the water's edge, the visitor finds an area of peaty ground now planted with electric-blue meconopsis, trilliums and the very best acid-loving shrubs and trees (magnolias, rhododendrons, azaleas and enkianthus). Magnificent trees reach for the sky, while ferns adore the conditions lower down, as does *Mertensia virginica*, the Virginian bluebell.

The garden suffered during the great storms of 1987 and 1990, but the damage provided new opportunities as previously canopied areas became bathed in sunlight. Today, dappled light falls through the extensive foliage and flickers over the sheets of water.

It was always Spedan Lewis's wish that the garden should be open to visitors, and – not surprisingly – from its very beginning it has been the partners who have been welcomed most regularly. But he also wanted to share it with a wider public through regular charitable openings. Visitors in turn still share it most days with kingfishers, water voles and other wildlife that delight in the atmosphere of calm. The water vole is now an endangered species, perhaps to the relief of the gardeners, who have a constant battle protecting the ancient royal ferns (*Osmunda regalis*) and the banks of the lakes from their gnawing.

Robert Ballard says that it is inevitable that the garden is more manicured now than it would have been in the past. He believes, however, that it still has the spirit of the place Spedan Lewis loved. Ballard is only the third head gardener since work began on the garden in 1946, and he relishes the pleasure the garden gives to its visitors. He is also enormously proud of the fact that the garden has been voted Finest Water Garden in the World by the International Waterlily & Water Gardening Society, as, surely, its creator would have been, too.

Candelabra primulas tumble into the water's edge. A world-class collection of water lilies thrives in the lakes of Longstock Water Garden.

Not many gardens that open to the public have a background of showbiz parties, with stars flying in by helicopter for raucous gatherings by the swimming pool. But that helps to explain the immediate popularity of the post-war charity openings of Dunsborough Park near Ripley in Surrey, then the home of the actress and comedienne Florence Desmond and her second husband, Charles Hughesdon.

The Hughesdons bought the estate in 1948 from the MP and aviation expert Oliver Simmonds, who worked on the gardens just before the Second World War, adding the greenhouses, ha-ha and pavilions. Beyond the ha-ha, the estate runs to some 3000 acres (1214 ha.) and reputedly includes six of the 100 oldest trees in England.

Immediately after the war, the house became the focal point for the Hughesdons' glamorous life-style, with guests including such royalty as the Duke of Edinburgh and such glamorous film stars as

Magnificent trees are a feature of Dunsborough Park.

The stone bridge and Ottoman-style viewing platform have been meticulously restored.

Elizabeth Taylor coming to the annual 'helicopter garden party'. Four or five times a year, at quieter times, the Hughesdons opened the gardens for charity, including for the NGS (beginning in 1950).

But it has been the current occupants of Dunsborough Park, Baron and Baroness Sweerts de Landas Wyborgh, who have transformed the estate. They have not only restored the garden to its former glory, but also taken it to a new level of beauty and sophistication.

The formal garden surrounds the house, a sixteenth-century farmhouse much extended in the eighteenth century. In a traditional style, the garden is made up of a series of 'rooms': a White Garden; a classic Italian garden with elegant statuary and water features, where now more sedate parties with opera and concert performances take place; an eighteenth-century walled garden lined on one side with large, white Edwardian greenhouses; and another walled garden recently redesigned by Caroline Sweerts as

A dusting of snow enhances the
statuary in the formal garden.

a sophisticated potager with a domed metal fruit cage at its centre. Legacies of previous garden plans are to be found throughout, such as a mulberry tree that is reputedly 300 years old.

Hidden behind shrubbery at the far edge of the formal garden is an ethereal water garden created from natural water sources in the 1930s. Part rock garden, part water garden, the dammed brook rushes to join the Ockham Mill stream and the River Wey, with rivulets of water tumbling over rocks, ferns nestling in damp crevices, and candelabra primulas leaning precariously over the water. Access to the other side is by small bridges, one of which is built of stone and has a covered, Ottoman-style viewing platform.

Another area has been devoted to roses, mostly old-fashioned varieties, which perfume the air. Every garden room is dressed with elegant statuary, the passion of Caroline's husband, Dolf. Each statue is given plenty of space, allowing visitors to enjoy them at their best, although the pieces change regularly as purchases come and go. Finally, a family garden, still with the infamous swimming pool and a grotto that used to have a tumbling fountain, provides a gentle antidote to the formality closer to the house.

Other touches, such as beautiful metal gates in the shape of a peacock's tail, enhance the planting, which varies from packed borders to the classic statement of four quince trees in a square on a simple lawn. Elsewhere, an unusual hedge of *Ginkgo biloba* frames a path.

The restoration of the garden was a mammoth undertaking, and it took five years to re-establish the structure. The Sweerts brought in the leading designer and plantswoman Penelope Hobhouse to help with the planning of the garden rooms. Later contributions were made by the gardens expert Rupert Golby and the landscape architect Simon Johnson. The enormous greenhouses – 148 feet (45 m) long and 20 feet (6 m) high – have been restored, but will probably not be so again, so great was the cost. Nevertheless, there is a romantic quality about them that conjures up the days when they were dripping with colourful orchids, and they still house a pomegranate tree brought from France in the early 1990s by Caroline and Dolf. The garden is now maintained by a team of four, with each person responsible for a different section of the garden in which they all take justifiable pride.

Precision-cut yew encloses the magnificent greenhouses.

Since it first opened to the public, in 1953, the garden at the Salutation, known as the Secret Gardens of Sandwich, Kent, has had a rollercoaster life, surviving several changes of ownership, an application for the house to be demolished, and the accumulation of 150 tonnes of dumped waste. Such a story is all the more astounding given the earlier history of the Salutation. Built on the site of an inn of that name, the Grade I-listed house was commissioned by the solicitor Henry Farrer in 1911, to be designed by his friend the eminent garden designer Edwin Lutyens. The garden was influenced by Gertrude Jekyll, and is blessed with a rich soil deposited at the mouth of the River Stour as it meets the English Channel.

The sculptor Leonard Byng, who owned the property from 1948 until his death in 1977, first opened the garden for the NGS in 1953. It was described in 1962 by the American landscape

An early view of the Grass Walk planting at the Salutation.

Pillars of *Quercus ilex* are underplanted with old-fashioned roses in the early 1960s (see also photograph opposite, bottom).

The long Grass Walk borders are seen at their summer peak.

architect Lanning Roper as 'a series of highlights … a garden of colour, of flowers and fragrance' (*Country Life*, 13 September 1962).

The garden has recently been magnificently restored by its current owners, the Parkers. Dominic Parker has calculated that thirty-five man-years of labour were needed to clear the garden of rubbish before it was replanted in the mid-2000s.

The initial surprise or 'secret' of this garden is that such a large garden exists in the middle of the small coastal town of Sandwich. One enters via the original herringbone brick paths, now relaid, between the long borders packed with a mix of annuals and exotic tender perennials. These include the rare Wollemi pine (*Wollemia nobilis*), as well as cannas, dahlias and other ever-changing tropical plants.

Passing long, densely planted herbaceous borders, the visitor soon catches sight of the small lake, originally dug in the 1970s. Around it, new

Areas for contemplative sitting
abound at the Salutation, the
'Secret Gardens'.

curved borders of shrubs and perennials have created areas of calm where one can sit and watch the wildlife.

Stretching out in front of the main broad terrace of the house is the lawned rose garden, which is still very much in the style of Jekyll, although she would not recognize the varieties now grown there. The long, rectangular borders have been replanted with pink roses of progressively deepening shades, including (appropriately) the vivid pink David Austin English rose 'Gertrude Jekyll' ('Ausbord'). The sequence ends with *Rosa* 'Rhapsody in Blue' ('Frantasia'), a new shrub rose that fades to a dusky maroon with age.

Vegetables are grown in a showpiece potager, while along the banks of the walled northern boundary gentle, winding paths lead through a woodland glade. This is brought to life in spring by carpets of wood anemones, honesty and the

Bergenias edge the path
to the bridge that leads to
an island, now restored.

white stems of such well-chosen shrubs as *Rubus cockburnianus* 'Goldenvale'.

Yet more delights are revealed as the garden opens out again and one passes through a wild-flower meadow planted with tens of thousands of fritillaries and species narcissi. At right-angles to the house, an avenue of almond trees (*Prunus dulcis*) interplanted with *Viburnum carlesii* 'Aurora' brings formality and structure while leading to the two final garden 'rooms', the White Garden and the Yellow Garden. All the paths are designed to have good views, and none is more charming than that of the circular White Garden. Gaps in the dense hedging create vistas of the elegant Bowling Lawn and allow glimpses of the more intimate Yellow Garden, as well as highlighting carefully placed sculptures.

With this density of planting, it is no surprise that the head gardener, Steve Edney, and his team of six helpers are kept busy. While much of the planting instigated by Leonard Byng in the 1950s – and so admired by Lanning Roper – has disappeared, the restoration work has remained true to the spirit of Jekyll, and has been helped by reference to photographs from both the 1900s and the 1960s. The garden was reopened to the public in 2007 by Monty Don.

In the late 1940s Margery Fish decided to write a book about her experience of creating a garden at her home, East Lambrook Manor in Somerset. It was to be called *Gardening with Walter*. However, Walter Fish died during its writing, and the idea was shelved, finally to be published in 1956 as *We Made a Garden*. It was no coincidence that this was also the first year that she opened her garden to the public through the NGS. According to her nephew Henry Boyd-Carpenter, she was a devotee of the scheme and always extremely proud to open for it. For an extra sixpence a head, she would take groups of visitors around the house. Boyd-Carpenter remembers regular weekends spent helping her on these open days. It was the start of his own commitment to the NGS, culminating in his position as one of its trustees for several years.

The NGS in turn was delighted to have such a seminal garden in *The Yellow Book*. Margery was not only an inspired gardener but also an accomplished writer, and the publication of her book confirmed her as one of Britain's best-loved and most influential gardeners of the mid-twentieth century. *We Made a Garden* tells the story of how she and her husband, Walter, bought East Lambrook Manor in 1937 and worked to create a garden from the poor, stony ground surrounding the fifteenth-century house. The book also tells of the clash of gardening styles pursued by the couple, Walter loving the formality of big mown lawns and regimented planting, and Margery scattering seed on the paving stones and hunting out long-forgotten cottage-garden plants that would soften the rigid edges.

By the mid-1950s Margery had not only become a successful gardening columnist, but also begun collecting and propagating the plants she was rediscovering: *Alchemilla*, *Astrantia*, *Dicentra*, primroses and many silver-leaved species. Such plants were not popular at a time when labour-intensive bedding was still the rage. Never

concerned with horticultural fashions, she made it her mission to find and propagate these plants, and the relatively modest manor-house garden was soon packed with her treasures.

While Margery did not set out to open a nursery, it was a natural progression given that her books and talks quickly increased the popularity of the cottage-garden style she promoted. Her visitors were desperate to take home some of the plants they saw growing, whether it was one of the rare older forms of double-flowering primrose (hose-in-hose or Jack-in-the-green) or the campanulas she used for ground cover, abhorring

Page 94, top
Margery Fish enhanced the natural water features at East Lambrook Manor with close planting on both banks.

Page 94, bottom
Narrow paths in local stone lure the visitor past dense planting.

Previous page
Euphorbias remain a hallmark of Margery Fish's cottage-garden style.

Below
Successive owners have maintained the spirit of the original planting that surrounded the fifteenth-century house.

The relaxed style of planting is a natural companion to the mellow Somerset stone.

the bare ground found in the stiff beds of hybrid roses of the time.

Seven more books followed *We Made a Garden*, and Margery continued to work in the garden, run the nursery and open the garden to visitors with the help of her nephew Henry until her death in 1969. After that, Henry maintained a legal career while looking after the garden and running the nursery at weekends. His parents lived in the manor house until their health declined, and in the mid-1980s the difficult decision was made to find a suitable buyer for the property.

Thankfully for the future of East Lambrook Manor, the new occupiers, the Nortons, were keen not only to revive the garden but also to catalogue its many plants and re-find missing varieties loved by Margery. After fifteen years they sold the property to the Williams family, who took the work of restoring the garden and developing the famous nursery even further. Much clearing needed to be done, as shrubs had outgrown their positions and perennials had swamped their beds.

The head gardener, Mark Stainer (who has been at East Lambrook since 1975), and his team continue to use Margery's books to re-create areas in the spirit of her beloved cottage-garden style. East Lambrook Manor is now occupied by Gail and Mike Werkmeister, and the garden and nursery not only thrive but also host horticultural courses. The Werkmeisters are no strangers to the NGS: they opened their previous garden, in Wimbledon, for several years, and knew they were up to the task.

It is indeed daunting to take over a garden that has opened for the NGS for many years. Lexham Hall in Norfolk, which has opened for the scheme for thirty years, was quite an inheritance for Neil and Anthea Foster, who took on the property in 1989. But the transition has been seamless and extremely successful.

The hall was built in about 1700 and suffered greatly in the early twentieth century. It was in a sorry state when it was bought by Anthea Foster's parents-in-law, William and Jean Foster, in 1946. While the extensive parkland was relatively unscathed, the formal garden surrounding the house had been completely destroyed during the Second World War.

The Fosters immediately began a campaign of restoration, and brought in the architect James Fletcher-Watson to remodel the hall. Rubble from a demolished Victorian extension was used to create the sweeping terrace to the south of the

building. The ha-ha was also excavated at this stage, creating the marvellous long pastoral views across the lake.

Jean Foster was responsible for the design and replanting of the formal garden. She had consulted the distinguished landscape architect Dame Sylvia Crowe, but when the plans arrived they were too elaborate, and only the positioning of the yew hedges was implemented. Jean was to prove an outstanding plantswoman in her own right; within nine years the garden had reached a standard high enough for *The Yellow Book*, and its regular openings began in 1956.

Visitors arrive first at the formal garden. In front of the terrace stretch long beds of roses, replanted in 1996–97 by Richard Beales, son of the famous Norfolk rose-grower Peter Beales, with scented, repeat-flowering specimens. The Long Walk, which has dense planting along one side, leads into the romantic woodland garden

Below
The south front of Lexham Hall, showing Fletcher-Watson's remodelled bay and Dutch gable.

Opposite, top
The long terrace planting, seen here in early summer, was designed by Jean Foster.

Opposite, bottom
Low box hedging mirrors the crinkle-crankle wall in the formal garden.

with its fine specimens of spring-flowering rhododendrons, azaleas and camellias. Among the superb magnolias are *M. campbellii*, *M. salicifolia*, *M. cylindrica*, *M. obovata* and *M. wilsonii*, with its heavenly scent. A natural stream connects with the River Nar, which runs through the estate, and is edged in spring with candelabra primulas and ferns.

Specimen trees were planted throughout the garden by the Fosters during their restoration of the estate, and now a new generation reaps the rewards of the magnificent *Paulownia tomentosa* (foxglove tree), *Sequoiadendron giganteum* (giant redwoods; some of them more than 130 feet/40 m high), *Davidia involucrata* (handkerchief tree) and *Cercidiphyllum japonicum* (katsura tree). Not all settled in smoothly; the Judas tree (*Cercis siliquastrum*) survived being moved twice before finally finding a happy situation.

While Jean Foster oversaw the planting, William Foster concentrated on improving the hard landscaping and putting in the small bridges over the streams and river. The charming nineteenth-century summer house in the woodland garden was restored, as was the tennis pavilion. A swimming pool was installed, well hidden by high hedging for privacy.

The part-walled vegetable garden is bounded on one side by a seventeenth-century crinkle-crankle wall. In a clever planning twist, the beds and planting along the other wall reflect these curves, giving extra shelter for such rare climbers as *Dregea sinensis*. This garden has been gradually made less labour-intensive by Anthea, with perennial beds edging the long path that crosses the central feature, a new arbour by the farrier Nigel Barnett, which will eventually be covered by *Wisteria floribunda* 'Yae-kokuryu' (also known as 'Black Dragon').

As was her mother-in-law before her, Anthea is a keen flower-arranger. However, she is not religious about colour coordination in flowerbeds, preferring to match shape and texture. She has also taken up the mantle of Jean's dedication to the NGS by becoming the County Organizer for Norfolk. The family is extremely proud of its long record of near-continuous openings since 1956.

Because of her involvement with the scheme, Anthea Foster is only too aware that the vagaries of the weather can cause upsets with opening schedules. Rare snow can cause hiccups with the garden's first opening each February, when snowdrops carpet the woodland garden. There are no such problems in May, the peak period for viewing the garden, when the glorious colours and scents of the rhododendrons, azaleas and magnolias are at their best at Lexham Hall.

By the River Nar, which meanders through the Lexham estate, planting is kept informal and naturalistic.

By the late 1950s the NGS was welcoming a wide range of gardens into *The Yellow Book*, including several in London. Also opening across the country were new gardens that had been created since the end of the Second World War. Few, however, were as ambitious in their scope as that made at Marwood Hill in the valley folds of north Devon by Dr Jimmy Smart.

In 1949 Dr Smart took up a post as a general practitioner and anaesthetist in Barnstaple. He bought a nearby property, Marwood House, which came with a seriously neglected garden. Smart set to work restoring it, but it soon became clear that it was not the ideal site for his ambitious plans. Although the garden was good enough to be opened for the NGS in 1958, when the opportunity arose in the early 1960s to buy more land across the road from his home, Smart leapt at it.

This was the start of the creation of one of the West Country's most magical gardens. Before long, Smart took the unusual step of building a house in the new garden, tailoring it to his planting passion rather than the other way round. The split-level building nestles on the side of the valley, giving views across and down the garden.

It was at this time that Malcolm Pharaoh arrived from Wisley to work as Smart's head gardener. Together they dammed a stream to create two small lakes, and transformed the former pastureland across the road into a lush plantation of some of the world's rarest shrubs. Smart was a keen propagator, and came back from visits to the United States with camellia cuttings that have now matured to form one of the world's finest collections.

When Smart retired, in 1973, the planting moved up a gear as more land was added. The final addition (in 1977) was a bank of land on the other side of the lakes, which gives visitors long views not only back towards the original garden but also on to the moors beyond. It has also provided space for seedling camellias that may or may not turn out to be winners, such as

Below
At Marwood Hill, twenty years' patience has been rewarded by the magnificent flowers now produced by *Magnolia sprengeri* 'Marwood Spring'.

Opposite, top
Far-reaching views look across the deep valley of the garden to the moors beyond.

Opposite, bottom
The westerly slopes of the garden were the final parcel of land to be added, in 1977.

The lower water garden at Marwood Hill is a haven for wildlife throughout the year.

A bronze of Sir Jimmy Smart by the sculptor Alan Biggs was unveiled as a millennium tribute in 2000.

the variety named after the garden's creator, *C. 'Jimmy Smart'*.

When one grows such shrubs as camellias and magnolias from seed or cuttings, patience is needed, but the rewards can be great. In front of the doctor's house is a magnolia specimen that took twenty years to flower. Smart's gamble paid off, and the tree, now named *M. sprengeri* 'Marwood Spring', is smothered with maroon flowers each spring.

Smart's obsession with plants continued, and his collections grew. The garden's National Collections of astilbe and *Iris ensata* suit the beautiful bog areas, while the tulbaghias show off the diversity of the various microclimates in the garden. The Upper Garden and scree bed house treasures more suited to drier, well-drained areas, including a variety of *Clianthus puniceus* (lobster claw) that is now extinct in its native New Zealand.

One of the few concessions to labour saving has been the sowing of prairie-style annuals on the south-facing side of the valley. Here, a spiral of naturalistic log benches beneath elegant birches provides views across the conservation area, which is planted with wild flowers and left uncut to encourage butterflies and bees for pollination.

Such is the diversity of plant life throughout the garden's 20 acres (8 ha.) that one may well be lucky enough to see a pair of kingfishers or some dragonflies darting over the fish-filled lakes. The variety of plants makes this a quite exceptional garden. That so many visitors return again and again is a fitting tribute to the doctor's passion.

It was always Smart's intention to share the garden with the public. Since his death in 2002, this wish has been perpetuated by the creation of a trust led by his nephew John Snowdon. Pharaoh continues to welcome visitors and answer their questions from the propagating shed that was built on his arrival at Marwood in the early 1970s.

1960–79
Years of Transition

Vanessa Berridge

The 1960s got under way with a swing. As it progressed, the decade was marked by a generally freer and less reverential spirit, which was gradually reflected in gardening. Russell Page's *The Education of a Gardener*, first published in 1962, was a Janus-like book: it evoked an earlier, more formal period, yet Page's advocacy of native plants, successional planting and drifts of naturalized bulbs and perennials influenced the designer and writer Rosemary Verey as she made her garden at Barnsley House in Gloucestershire during the 1960s.

Page also anticipated the work of such gardeners as Beth Chatto and John Brookes, who were to set the tone for gardening throughout the next two decades. Both valued plants more for their shape and texture, and chose them for the conditions in which they would flourish rather than forcing them into pre-determined and artificial schemes. Gardens became places for use, rather than static pictures, while the work of the

American landscape architect Lanning Roper suggested that cottage plants could be used successfully in small town gardens. With an increase in affluence and home-ownership, gardening was now the pastime of the many. Radio and television played their part in its growing popularity, with the much-loved Percy Thrower presenting *Gardeners' World* from 1969 to 1976. Harold Wilson's 'white heat of technology' meant there were new aids for amateur gardeners, such as polythene cloches and propagators; the Flymo made its appearance in 1966. By 1970 the annual turnover of the horticultural industry was more than £100 million.

The 1970s marked an increased interest in naturalistic planting. The droughts of 1975 and 1976 forced gardeners to rethink how and what they planted, while the BBC television series *The Good Life*, which ran from 1975 to 1978, poked fun at – but also flagged up the move towards – self-sufficiency. This at first quaint-seeming concept stalled after the election of Margaret Thatcher in 1979, but would gather momentum three decades later with concerns over climate change. Many gardening ideas that are now regarded as axiomatic were first tried out during the tumultuous decades of the 1960s and 1970s.

A garden that first opened early in this period was Docwra's Manor in Cambridgeshire. A friend of Faith Raven's mother was an organizer for the National Gardens Scheme, so it was inevitable that Faith and her husband, John, would open their house for the scheme. They did so for the first time in 1962, some eight years after they had moved in. The main body of the house is from the seventeenth century, with an eighteenth-century facade. Wisteria, a self-sown rose and a vine clamber up this gracious frontage, with a *Prunus* 'Shogetsu' (*P. longipes*) appearing through a yew to one side. Eighteenth-century iron railings divide the garden from the road, and a path leading to the

door is edged with standard *Rosa* 'Albéric Barbier'. The garden, which was originally 1½ acres (0.6 ha.), is now about an acre larger, the house having been reunited in the 1960s with the barns and land that once surrounded it as a working farm. Two courtyard gardens (one paved, the other of gravel) have been created in the former farmyards.

The garden has grown organically and at its own pace over the years. The old farmyard walls have been extended by hedges of yew and beech and by cordons of apples, enclosing different areas, each with its own personality. Much of the garden is naturally ebullient, and the owners' love of plants triumphs over formality, except at the front of the house. After almost sixty years, the garden is filled with personal memories. An early twentieth-century temple, standing between a holly and a yew on the main lawn, was a gift from King's College, Cambridge, where John Raven was a Fellow in Classics. Tucked among evergreen shrubs and hardy geranium ground cover is a

turret from the chapel of King's. An old box tree, once a hiding place for the Ravens' son, has more recently been clipped into Japanese-style cloud topiary by the part-time gardener, David Aitchison.

When the Ravens moved to Docwra's in 1954, shortly after their marriage, they started with the front borders, and then laid to lawn what had been a vegetable garden outside the kitchen. Throughout the 1960s and 1970s, before his untimely death in 1980, John Raven was deeply involved in the garden, and, as a keen botanist, put his mark on the planting. A feature in the early days was *Tulipa saxatilis* Bakeri Group (*T. bakeri*), which he had brought back from the southern Mediterranean before the Second World War, and which was tenderly nursed by his aunt during the war years.

The Ravens continued to gather seeds and cuttings (scrupulously and legitimately) from all over Europe. A *Clematis cirrhosa* from southern France grows like a curtain over a barn. In a corner of the paved garden is a rare alchemilla from

northern Italy, and in a raised bed elsewhere is *Cardamine enneaphylla* from Turkey.

On the whole, however, fewer Mediterranean plants are now grown, because although they cope with the East Anglian drought in summer, they fare less well during winter frosts. So Faith has moved towards introducing more native wild plants to the garden, always focusing on species rather than hybrids. Recently, she has started counting them: expecting to find about fifty, she discovered more than 300 British natives, many encouraged by self-seeding.

This is a luxuriant, plant-packed garden, in which box roundels and pyramids are but occasional exclamation marks among billowing summer perennials in the walled garden. Walls are softened by climbing roses and clematis, while cordons of apples are a transparent barrier between the paved garden and the orchard. Through a wild area runs an avenue of 'Fritz Nobis' roses, glimpsed between the branches of a bumpy yew hedge from the path beyond.

The colours throughout are muted, with pastel shades of yellow, apricot and blue offset by grey Mediterranean foliage. The achieved aim is understatement. No understatement, however, is the proud boast in *The Yellow Book* that the garden has opened for the NGS for more than forty years.

The flowers of sweet rocket (*Hesperis matronalis*), flowing through various irises, pick up the shape and shade of *Crambe cordifolia* in the walled garden at Docwra's Manor.

Gardens are places where I can breathe and relax, admire the perfection of the designer's eye and absorb the sounds and scents of drunken insects and nature's own perfumes.

Fiona Reynolds, former Director-General of the National Trust

Spires of peach eremurus soar upwards through a billowing veil of *Crambe cordifolia* above a mound of hardy purple geraniums.

An avenue of 'Fritz Nobis' roses runs through the wild garden, where the grass is left deliberately long.

A garden created over a similarly long period of time, but in two distinct stages, is the 4-acre (1.6-ha.) Denmans in West Sussex. It is the creation of two people, the late Mrs Joyce Robinson and, more recently, the landscape designer and writer John Brookes. Denmans was once the garden to a country house. Mrs Robinson and her husband bought the land in 1946 because it was adjacent to their farm. Its proximity to a busy road caused problems with farming, so they began growing strawberries, as well as cut flowers for the London market. After the death of her husband, Mrs Robinson made Denmans into a decorative garden, and, wanting to share her joy in gardening with others, opened for the first time for the NGS in 1967.

Mrs Robinson was much influenced in the 1960s and 1970s by Sir Frederick Stern, who gardened on chalk at nearby Highdown. She adopted the plant-led style of gravel gardening that has since been popularized by Beth Chatto and by the Savill Garden in Windsor Great Park. It was Mrs Robinson who made the dry gravel stream at Denmans; it is now filled with self-seeded verbascum, sedums and *Alchemilla mollis*, and winds its way through the garden to a pool, since added by Brookes.

Apart from a walled flower garden, through which visitors now enter, there are no hard and fast divisions within the garden, and constant glimpses are offered of fields, copses and Fontwell racecourse. Set within the garden are a converted gardener's cottage and an eighteenth-century stable block with a clock tower, where Brookes now lives.

Lawns flow round these two buildings and around plantings of trees, shrubs and perennials, chosen so that between them they give year-round interest. Mown grass paths snake through areas of longer grass, full of bulbs in spring, and cut just once a fortnight in summer to give a two-tiered definition to the garden.

John Brookes, formerly a director of the Inchbald School of Design in London, had brought students to the garden in the 1970s. When he was looking for a new direction in the early 1980s, he moved to Denmans to help Mrs Robinson, who was suffering increasingly from rheumatism. Although he admired her as a plantswoman, he felt that, as a designer, he could build on what she had started. For him, line and texture are more important than colour, which, he says, is just a bonus.

Brookes chooses strong shapes, including trees with interesting bark, such as *Acer griseum*. A bed of *Helenium* 'Moerheim Beauty' and *Perovskia* 'Blue Spire' is backed with architectural grasses; banks of white *Hydrangea arborescens* 'Annabelle' are mixed with claret astrantias; and bright-orange dahlias are grouped so that they jut out into the lawn like the prow of a ship. Fringing a round pond on the top lawn are some tender species, *Acer palmatum* 'Sango-Kaku' ('Senkaki')

Previous pages
The flower garden is still punctuated with large mushrooms of box; at its centre is an oil jar with grey-leafed *Astelia chathamica* at its base.

Left
The tall grey spires of *Verbascum bombyciferum* contrast with green flowers of *Alchemilla mollis* as part of loose mixed planting in gravel.

Below, left
Foxgloves (*Digitalis purpurea*) beneath a belichened Judas tree (*Cercis siliquastrum*) on the main lawn.

Below
Throughout the garden at Denmans, plant forms are as important as colour. In the walled garden, spiky sisyrinchium, stachys and foxgloves contrast with a soft dome of purple sage.

and a rare myrtle (*Myrtus apiculata* syn. *Luma apiculata*). Key trees in the garden include silver birches, a towering metasequoia, a whitebeam, two red oaks and a multi-stemmed, belichened Judas tree (*Cercis siliquastrum*). All are underplanted with a band of evergreen shrubs, backing the sinuous beds and protecting the garden from southwesterly winds.

The garden still opens for the NGS on one day in March, but the major change since the 1980s has been its transformation from private to public garden, with the farmyard converted into shops, teashop and nursery. In 2009 Brookes overhauled the walled garden, which had become shrubby and overgrown. The gravel running through here links this more compartmentalized area with the rest of the less formal garden. But the walled garden, too, has a glorious profusion of planting, with a papery-flowered *Romneya coulteri*, asters, heleniums, eucomis, veronicastrum, lysimachia, agapanthus and echiums, as well as clipped box and a central weeping copper beech. The delight of Denmans is that this expansive garden of lawns, sprawling beds and tall trees nevertheless offers spaces that visitors can relate to, and is full of ideas for smaller gardens.

Visitors to Hodsock Priory in Nottingham-shire enter through a majestic gatehouse of 1490, flanked by two imposing *Viburnum tinus*. In early spring, when the garden is at its peak, the banks of the moat are a mass of snowdrops, aconites and *Helleborus foetidus*. Sir Andrew and Lady Buchanan inherited Hodsock from his aunt in 1967 only to discover that they were committed to opening the garden for the NGS on the May bank holiday. With a house emptied of furniture, no money and three young children, it was a daunting prospect, but somehow they managed.

Hodsock, which has never actually been a priory, has been in Sir Andrew's family since 1765. Between the wars it had had a famous garden, tended by six full-time gardeners. Sir Andrew believes that both house and garden were saved from destruction by the fact that they were taken over in the Second World War not by 'licentious soldiery' but by the Land Army. Nevertheless,

keeping the garden going in the immediate aftermath of the war was a challenge for his aunt and uncle, who concentrated on the central terrace and wide Fan Lawn (so-called because of the shape of its beds), on show to the public in 1967.

The after-effects of war were still felt at that time. Lady Buchanan took on responsibility for the 5½-acre (2.2-ha.) formal garden, but the couple struggled to maintain it, pressing their weekend visitors into donning wellies and lending a hand. The NGS played an indirect but crucial role in transforming the garden's fortunes two decades later, in the late 1980s. Kate Garton, a recent horticulture graduate in search of a job, wrote to all Nottinghamshire garden openers in *The Yellow Book*. The Buchanans, the only people who replied to her letter, took her on as head gardener.

Clearing the dense undergrowth beneath the 300-year-old oaks in Horsepasture Wood, Kate found traces of an ornamental path, and, beside it, blankets of the double snowdrop *Galanthus nivalis* 'Flore Pleno'. Almost certainly planted in the nineteenth century, they reflected the Victorian fashion for woodland walks. Hodsock has since become known for its snowdrops, opening since 1990 throughout February, and continuing to make an annual donation to the NGS. The collection has grown: 250,000 more snowdrops were planted in 2000, and existing clumps are separated 'in the green' (immediately after flowering) every year, and replanted to fill gaps.

Although the snowdrops are the major attraction, the garden offers much to the late-winter visitor in terms of colour and fragrance. The double snowdrops have been planted in narrow borders through the fan-shaped beds of the main lawn, and are followed in late February by the early-flowering *Narcissus* 'Tête-à-Tête'. There are banks of yellow aconites and *Helleborus argutifolius*, and of the honey-scented *Galanthus* 'S. Arnott'. The bare trunks of deciduous trees are

underplanted with pink *Cyclamen coum*, while further winter interest comes from the snakebark maple, *Acer pensylvanicum*. Paths wind between low hedges of sarcococca (Christmas box) and scented winter-flowering honeysuckle (*Lonicera × purpusii*).

The main lawn is bordered by a hedge of holm oak (*Quercus ilex*) and by a lake fringed with yellow *Cornus mas* and the snow-white branches of *Rubus cockburnianus* 'Goldenvale'. Other delights of winter colour and scent include *Chimonanthus praecox* and the star-shaped flowers of *Viburnum × bodnantense* 'Dawn'.

Rare snowdrop cultivars, several of them named after female ancestors of Sir Andrew, stud a terraced bank by the moat, part of the waterworks that frame this wonderful wintry garden. Horsepasture Wood is still carpeted with 'Flore Pleno', linking a constantly evolving garden with its Victorian past.

Top
On a misty winter's morning, the priory and the stems of five white silver birches (*Betula utilis* var. *jacquemontii*) are reflected in the glassy surface of the lake.

Above
Snowdrops are a great attraction for visitors in February, and are planted with other winter delights, including hellebores and purple ericas.

A garden with a somewhat shorter history is that of York Gate in West Yorkshire, the work of two generations of Spencers. Fred Spencer, a chartered surveyor, bought the stone-built Victorian house in 1951 as a family home on the outskirts of Leeds. With an acre of land, the former farmhouse seemed ideal for Fred and his wife, Sybil, who were both keen gardeners. Fred began laying down the basic structure, with divisions of yew and beech hedging, but it was the Spencers' son, Robin – only sixteen when the family moved to York Gate – who was to be the creative genius of the garden until his premature death at the age of forty-seven in 1982.

Opening for the NGS for the first time in 1968, York Gate was very much a garden of that period. The Spencers were among the first generation of post-war middle-class professionals, who actually made their own gardens rather than employing others to do it for them.

York Gate now belongs to a charity. It was previously the home of two generations of the Spencer family, who were responsible for the design and layout of the garden.

The Herb Garden is the most formal area of York Gate, with impact created mainly by the contrasting greens of topiary. A pot of bright tulips introduces a flash of colour in May.

A gravel path leads through the Herb Garden to the arcaded summer house. In summer, the box roundels and helter-skelter topiary are interspersed with purple alliums.

Designed by Robin Spencer, the Pavement Maze is made with reclaimed granite setts, reflecting its creator's interest in the Arts and Crafts Movement.

The chief phase of creativity at York Gate was in the 1960s and 1970s, and elements of the garden still recall those decades. The alpine scree bank and alpine troughs in the Paved Garden, for instance, are typical 1960s features. Recently, David Beardall, head gardener since 2001, found *Onopordum nervosum* (*O. arabicum*) when he was double-digging. He had never previously spotted it in the garden, and is sure that it was planted by either Robin or Sybil Spencer, so characteristic is it of 1970s flower arrangements.

With his exceptional eye for detail, Robin created an original and outstanding small garden. Each of a dozen different garden 'rooms' has its own distinctive character. A follower of the Arts and Crafts Movement, he used local materials to artistic effect in many different places. The two-dimensional Pavement Maze is made from reclaimed granite setts, and visually breaks up the gravel drive that originally led to the garage. In the

In June, the half-standards of *Rosa* 'White Pet' in the white and silver border at York Gate are in full flower, surrounded by clouds of *Geranium clarkei* 'Kashmir White' and *Lychnis coronaria* 'Alba'.

The hot colours of the front border stand in marked contrast to the pastel tones that prevail elsewhere in the garden. Planting here includes *Helenium* 'Moerheim Beauty', the dark-leafed dahlias 'Bishop of Llandaff' and 'David Howard', *Crocosmia* 'Lucifer' and, at the back, the yellow *Clematis* 'Bill MacKenzie'.

Damp-lovers, such as hostas and primulas, flourish in the Woodland Dell, a cool haven through which a stream flows from the orchard pond.

The Nut Walk links the garden with the countryside beyond.

Paved Garden, the risers within the different levels of paving are also stone setts, taken from the former farmyard.

There are echoes, too, of the former farm in the orchard, where just one apple tree remains from before the Spencers owned the house. There, Fred made a pond and a stream, the latter running into the Woodland Dell. The dell is planted with damp-loving hostas, primulas, *Beesia calthifolia* and rare native orchids. In pleasing contrast to the informality of the orchard and dell is the Arts and Crafts Herb Garden, with spirals and roundels of box, and gravel and brick paths.

Elsewhere, a shady, dry border of ferns is tucked beneath clipped 15-foot (4.5-m) triangles of yew, designed to look like sails. In summer, the climbing nasturtium, *Tropaeolum speciosum*, scrambles through this dark topiary. The nasturtium's fiery red is picked up in a hot border planted with *Helenium* 'Moerheim Beauty', yellow 'Bill MacKenzie' clematis, dark-leafed *Dahlia* 'Bishop of Llandaff' and *Crocosmia* 'Lucifer'. Yet another contrast can be found in the white and silver border, with its half-standards of *Rosa* 'White Pet' surrounded by *Lychnis coronaria* 'Alba' and white geraniums.

There is also a nut walk, underplanted with the sweetly scented *Galanthus* 'S. Arnott', which leads to Sybil's Garden. For many years chairman of the local horticultural society, Sybil died in 1994, leaving York Gate to Perennial, the Gardeners' Royal Benevolent Society, confident that the society would maintain and cherish the garden, and would continue to open it for the NGS. No garden stands still, of course, and the rockery in Sybil's Garden, which had become overgrown, was redesigned in 2004 using grasses, hardy ground-cover geraniums, *Cirsium rivulare* and cardoons for architectural effect. It strikes a more contemporary note, yet picks up on the circular theme so consistently used by Robin Spencer. It is a satisfying blend of the old and the new.

In recent years, small town gardens opening for the NGS have multiplied, but for the first four or five decades most listings in *The Yellow Book* were of larger, country gardens. Lady Amabel Lindsay's garden at 12 Lansdowne Road, London, was, therefore, an exception, opening for the first time for the scheme in 1970. Lady Amabel was then on an NGS committee responsible for finding and nominating gardens, and modestly suggests that this was the reason she put hers forward.

The front garden is an earnest of what is to come, and its planting themes are carried through to the 100-foot-long (30 m) plot behind the house. The door of the grey-brick, late Regency-style house is approached by a flagstone path edged on both sides by a narrow border of hellebores, aquilegia, hardy geraniums and dianthus, lending interest from February to late summer. A tree-canopied bank planted with lilac, *Hydrangea arborescens* 'Annabelle', *Verbena*

bonariensis and lavender rises up to one side. Facing it is a bank of the repeat-flowering *Rosa* 'Pearl Drift', backed by a hedge of Christmas box (sarcococca), which fills the air with scent in February. Pots of architectural hostas stand like sentinels by the front door and appear again on the terrace at the back of the house, along with tender pelargoniums, datura and fuchsia.

Standing on this terrace, it is hard to believe that the garden is only a block away from a busy London thoroughfare, for it is a haven of rural peace. Towering limes and a *Robinia pseudoacacia* 'Frisia' in neighbouring gardens, together with clematis-covered trellising, blur the boundaries and give the impression of a much larger garden. This effect is heightened by the layout, which was in place when the Lindsays moved to the house in 1962. It works so well that Lady Amabel saw no need to change it, enabling her to open the garden with confidence within eight years.

An irregularly shaped lawn swirls around a multi-stemmed mulberry, which lies almost prostrate across the garden, concealing what is behind. The lawn then disappears around another bed, dominated by a large pyramidal bay tree, to join a stone path across the back of the garden. The mulberry is centuries old and may well have been planted by the Pembroke family, which once owned the estate on which the house stands.

Plants including sarcococca, 'Annabelle' hydrangeas, pale-pink roses and *Verbena bonariensis* are repeated through the beds. There is a period feel to the style of the garden, which features individual favourites, planted to emphasize their attributes rather than in the large drifts that are so popular today. These individuals include a bluey-purple abutilon, red chard grown for its looks as much as for eating, and intertwined clematis and sweet peas on two red metal tripods at the centre of the main border.

Other highlights are a waxy-leafed *Ceanothus* ×
delileanus 'Gloire de Versailles' against the back
fence and a pergola, usually covered with wisteria
in May. With the inevitable limitations of a
compact planting area, Lady Amabel faces the
annual anxiety as to whether the garden will be at
its peak when she opens during the Chelsea
Flower Show, usually the last week in May.

The garden has changed relatively little since
1962. A weeping elm near the house has been
replaced with a heavily fruiting crab apple, and
the greenhouse has recently been doubled in
size to provide a winter home for summer
pots. Pelargoniums are trained against the wall
inside, and flourish in the deep trench specially
made for them.

Tree peonies are kept in pots so that they can
be moved to prominent positions during their
short flowering season, and hidden away at other
times. This is just one of the clever tricks of a
garden full of ideas and interest for those who
struggle to create big effects in a small space.

A neighbouring yellow-green
Robinia pseudoacacia 'Frisia'
towers above the Victorian-style
greenhouse at 12 Lansdowne
Road, year-round home
to scented pelargoniums.
An ancient mulberry tree is
the focal point of the garden.

The 1960s were a turning point for British gardening, and the chief architect of change was Beth Chatto, who remains, in 2012, its First Lady. She forsook what had become the classic English-woman's garden of formal rooms and billowing herbaceous borders for a much more naturalistic way of gardening, which worked with the grain of the land. In 1960 she and her husband, Andrew, moved to a house they had built on wasteland at the back of his family's fruit farm in Elmstead Market, Essex. The inhospitable hollow below was filled with deposits of gravel, clay, silt and sand left by a melting glacier during the last ice age. The annual rainfall here is one of the lowest in the country, and higher up there are areas so arid that even native weeds curl up and die in summer; yet elsewhere the soil is 'soggy and boggy', in Beth's words, while three-hundred-year-old oak trees and ancient hedgerows create large patches of dry shade. Although she says that it seemed mad at the time to want to make a garden in such a place, she

was undaunted by these problems, and set about creating what has become one of the finest examples of late twentieth-century gardening.

Influences included the local artist Sir Cedric Morris, who introduced Beth to species plants, such as alliums and fritillaries, then unseen in nurseries and garden centres. Her husband's interest in the origins of plants encouraged her to choose the right plant for the right situation, whether dry, wet or shady. Rather than shoe-horning plants into places where they would not flourish, she pioneered a new attitude to gardening, which is today taken almost for granted.

Within 5 acres (2 ha.), Beth has created many different garden areas, developing the site constantly over fifty years. One of her first endeavours, in the early 1960s, was the Mediterranean Garden, where clipped mounds of santolina and ballota grow on sandy slopes around a taller *Genista aetnensis* (Mount Etna broom). This area is now linked to the more recently

planted alpine-style scree beds on the south side of the house. Gravel paths eddy round curving island beds of alpines, laid out using a hosepipe and presided over by a Judas tree, *Cercis sili-quastrum*. Four large ponds, each slightly lower than the last, and separated by mown grass-covered banks, were made by damming a spring-fed ditch. These are lushly green from early summer until late autumn, with *Lysichiton americanus* followed by candelabra primulas and then the huge parasols of *Gunnera tinctoria*.

Beth also planted other trees in scale with the oaks, including a now massive weeping willow, a metasequoia, a Japanese larch and a paulownia. These were needed to provide an understorey for the garden at the outset, and to stop it from looking like farmland.

The hurricane of 1987 thinned out the woodland area, providing Beth with a chance to plant hostas, mahonia and the brilliantly red-stemmed *Cornus sanguinea* 'Midwinter Fire' in

what had become dappled shade. One of the garden's most significant developments took place in 1991, when a car park was converted into a gravel garden. English in its planting style, it has more than a hint of the Mediterranean thanks to its drought-loving plants, including santolina, lavender, eryngium, euphorbia and cistus. Uprights of yew, tall alliums and fennel give height, and lift visitors' eyes to the trees above.

Beth's commitment to bringing her planting philosophy to a wider public has been constant for many decades. In the late 1960s and early 1970s she began writing regularly about gardening for newspapers and magazines, and she published her first book, *The Dry Garden*, in 1978. Five years earlier, she had first opened for the NGS, charging just 20 pence for admission. And, in 1977, she won the first of ten consecutive Gold Medals for her exhibits at the Chelsea Flower Show. There, too, she was a pioneer, putting previously unfashionable hellebores, hostas and alliums on the horticultural map.

Shape, texture and form have always mattered as much to Beth as colour. Even in winter, plants rather than hard landscaping give character to a garden that remains at its core a living catalogue of the nursery Beth started in 1967, now world-famous.

If Beth Chatto's garden is renowned for its progressive approach to planting, the modern world vanishes as the visitor approaches Felley Priory down a long drive – although it is less than five minutes' drive from the M1 motorway. The priory was founded in 1156 and dissolved by Henry VIII in 1536, although traces of the monastic past remain. A high wall to the south-east, a good backdrop for tall shrubs, is thought to be part of the medieval boundary. The present house, built later in the sixteenth century, was given further solidity by additions in the 1880s.

There are terraced lawns, a pergola, a romantic rose garden and an abundance of shrubs and herbaceous perennials. Yew hedging with topiary gives the garden structure and creates a magnificent prospect on a snowy day. Against the house is a *Magnolia grandiflora* 'Exmouth', which flowers in August, while below on a terrace is a wisteria with a deep bole, and beyond that an ancient mulberry tree. Outside the walls of the formal garden are a meadow and shrubbery, where fritillaries flower when the garden opens for the NGS in April. Beyond is an unbroken view of the fields and hills of Nottinghamshire.

Felley has been owned by the Chaworth Musters family since 1822, but it was only in 1973 that Major Robert Chaworth Musters moved there from another ancestral home. The following year he married the Honourable Maria Monckton, and together they started turning the garden into the romantic and beautiful place it is today. At that point, it consisted of no more than a long, low yew hedge across the centre of the garden and four small rose beds. Yet within two years the Chaworth Musters were opening for the NGS, just as a shelter belt of yew went in to protect the double herbaceous borders from the fierce winds that would otherwise blow unchecked across the garden in winter.

Maria Chaworth Musters, who died in 2010, created what is very much an Englishwoman's

garden. Of necessity, it had to work commercially ('wash its face', in her words), and so, in the early 1990s, she opened a nursery to help ensure its survival. Nevertheless, the garden retains an intimacy typical of a period when such people as Rosemary Verey, Alvilde Lees-Milne and Penelope Hobhouse were working on their gardens, and making them personal gardening statements. These are gardens that mix formality with informality, looking both forward and back in design terms.

The nursery at Felley specializes in unusual plants, reflected in the range of planting through-out the garden itself. In one bed, for instance, are hydrangeas, including the oak-leafed *Hydrangea quercifolia* 'Snowflake' and *H. aspera* Kawakamii Group. In spring there are wallflowers and fritillaries, followed by tree peonies, *Parahebe perfoliata*, *Schisandra rubriflora* (which flowers in spring and autumn), *Viburnum plicatum* f. *tomentosum* 'Pink Beauty' and *Euphorbia rigida*, which changes from mauve to pink. Other special plants include *Drimys winteri*, *Clerodendrum bungei* and the majestic *Cardiocrinum giganteum*. The yew-backed double borders flower from May to October, with herbaceous staples including poppies, delphiniums, kniphofias, penstemons, phlox, potentilla, lobelia, thalictrum and achillea.

The house is now the home of Sophie and Victoria Brudenell, Major Chaworth Musters's granddaughters, and their father and stepmother. The garden has not stood still, however, since Maria's death. The rose garden, which was beginning to fade, was completely replanted in 2011. Thirty-five of Maria's favourite varieties (rather than the original eighty to a hundred) were planted in groups of three, to give a better show: a fitting tribute to the garden's creator.

Saling Hall in Essex is a late seventeenth-century brick house, one facade of which was covered with vines when the wine and gardens writer Hugh Johnson and his wife, Judy, first saw the property in 1971. To them, this seemed to be a good augury, as Hugh had just published *The World Atlas of Wine*. The garden, although overgrown, had lovely bones and was an enticement in itself. The Johnsons' predecessor, Lady Carlyle, had been an enthusiastic gardener before her eyesight failed in her late eighties, and in the late 1950s — at a time when few people would have undertaken anything so bold or forward-looking — she had planted large numbers of parrotias, metasequoias, liquid-ambars and taxodiums around a water garden.

An avenue of Lombardy poplars at the front of the house, also planted by Lady Carlyle, has been maintained, and those further away pruned more fiercely to make the row appear longer and the garden wider than it is. To one side of the house is the walled garden of 1698, where the Johnsons

replaced the collapsing topiary and, within a rigid framework, established a lavish mixture of shrubs, phlox, salvias, agapanthus and delphiniums. Apple trees, planted more than fifty years ago and pruned into parasols by Lady Carlyle, remain, and are described by Hugh Johnson as looking like nests of writhing serpents in winter.

In 1972 the Johnsons began their own programme of tree-planting, creating an arboretum with ponds and a cascade over the next two decades. The arboretum, now maturing well, was no more than a few sticks in a field when the couple first opened for the NGS in 1976. Lady Carlyle had previously opened the garden, but the Johnsons wanted time to put their own stamp on it before readmitting the public. Judy Johnson, who was actively involved in the NGS for many years, felt, like her husband, that opening was an enjoyable obligation that went with the ownership of a historic house and important garden.

Opposite, top
Hugh Johnson has planted
many trees in the garden at
Saling Hall, including
this *Amelanchier laevis*, in full
bloom in spring.

Opposite, bottom
The pillars of *Chamaecyparis
lawsoniania* 'Pottenii' were
planted in the Walled Garden
by Lady Carlyle, the Johnsons'
predecessor at Saling Hall. The
gnarled apple trees on each
side of the lawn have been
clipped as parasols for more
than fifty years.

Right
Hummocks of clipped box in
the arboretum reflect
Johnson's keen interest in
Japanese gardening.

Below
This stone folly is known as
the Temple of Pisces by Hugh
and Judy Johnson, who were
both born under that star sign.
It stands at the far end of the
arboretum from the house.

Visitors can now enjoy the fruits of more than five decades of almost continual planting. Beyond the walled garden, the visitor is led on, in eighteenth-century style, catching momentary glimpses along the way of statuary and other focal points, including a classical Temple of Pisces. There are glades, enclosed woodland areas and hidden gardens, including one in which cloud hedging of box surrounds a fine white mulberry. In a miniature French oak forest, trees are grown as close together as possible, and have long, straight stems.

Hugh Johnson has planted several pines: the ponderosa (*Pinus ponderosa*), the loblolly (*P. taeda*) and the big cone pine with branches like barbed wire, chosen because he particularly likes the savage look of California pines. The influence of his frequent visits to Japan can be seen in the Japanese-style hummocks of clipped box and in the Shinto gate, framed by the branches of four white birches (*Betula utilis* var. *jacquemontii* 'Jermyns') on a peninsula in one of the ponds.

The garden continues to evolve. To mark the new millennium, the Johnsons placed a block of granite in a yew chapel at the end of a long walk. And, after years of planting, they have begun to cut down trees, many of which had grown more than 2 metres as a result of a particularly wet summer.

Saling Hall is remarkable because, as Hugh Johnson says in his guidebook to it, much of the tradition of the English country house, its park and its pleasure grounds has been packed into the relatively small space of 12 acres (4.8 ha.).

As at Saling Hall, water is an important feature of Westbury Court, on the banks of the River Severn in Gloucestershire; in fact, this is a rare example in Britain of a Dutch seventeenth-century water garden. This style of gardening, popular during the reign of William and Mary (1689–1702), was short-lived, swept away by the eighteenth-century landscape movement. The exquisite, geometric garden of canals, yew hedging, and yew and box topiary is presided over by an elegant pavilion on stilts and a holm oak (*Quercus ilex*), planted in 1600 and probably the largest in the country.

The garden was begun in 1696 by Maynard Colchester, who had court connections, and was likely to have been influenced by a canal garden at nearby Flaxley Abbey, which was owned by a Dutch acquaintance. The Long Canal was dug out, and the flanking hedges and topiary were planted in 1699. Early in the next decade, the Tall Pavilion was built and furnished, and an ironwork clairvoyee made at the opposite end of the canal. The garden was enlarged a dozen years later by Colchester's nephew, who created the T-canal (which lies parallel to the Long Canal), constructed a second clairvoyee to the road, and erected the square

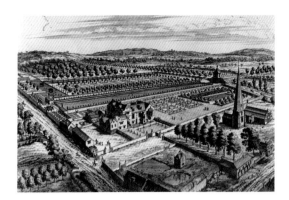

The engraving of 1707 of Westbury Court by Johannes Kip provided the National Trust with an invaluable guide when restoring the garden.

One of the Trust's first jobs was to replant the yew hedging, much of which had died.

This old photograph shows the ironwork clairvoyee to the road, probably made about 1714.

A mid-seventeenth-century
statue of Neptune stands in the
centre of the T-canal's top arm.

gazebo and adjoining small walled garden. He also rebuilt the house in Palladian style, although it was subsequently demolished in 1805.

The family then deserted Westbury until 1895, when they built another house on the site, although the garden was maintained in their absence – hence its survival to the present day. After various incarnations, the Victorian house was demolished by the local council, making Westbury into a further curiosity as a garden without a house. The advantage is, however, that you focus your attention on a unique piece of garden history as you wander past tranquil canals and between hedges of yew and box, and explore the formal walled garden and immaculate box parterre.

This history would not be visible were it not for the work of the National Trust, which took on Westbury in 1967 as its first major garden reconstruction. It was another ten years before the garden first opened on behalf of the NGS, with

which the Trust has always had a very close relationship. The first NGS opening marked the end of a decade that set the tone for future garden restorations both by the Trust and by other heritage organizations. Another ten years would elapse before an even more extensive reclamation was attempted by the Trust, this time on the great political landscape garden at Stowe in Buckinghamshire.

Westbury was indeed a significant endeavour, as it was near derelict in 1967, suffering from more than fifteen years of neglect. The canals had silted up and some hedges were overgrown, while others had died. Also to be addressed was the perennial problem of the low-lying garden being subject to flooding, affecting the yew hedges, which also suffer from the disease *Phytophthora ramoreum* (sudden oak death). Yet, looking today at the precise reflections of hedges and topiary in the glassy water of the canals, it is hard to believe this story of dilapidation.

The Tall Pavilion at Westbury Court was built between 1702 and 1703, and was reconstructed after the National Trust acquired the garden in 1967. It is seen above from the parterre across the T-canal. It stands at the top of the Long Canal, which is flanked by yew hedging and alternating yew pyramids and box balls, all reflected in the still water (opposite, top).

Opposite, bottom
The box parterre and a quincunx consisting of a *Phillyrea angustifolia* and four Portuguese laurels, clipped into mushrooms, are seen beneath the branches of thorn trees (*Crataegus crus-galli*).

Accurate reconstruction was made possible by records of the original plantings in the Gloucester archives, and by an engraving of 1707 by Johannes Kip. Another key feature, at either end of the box knot gardens, is a formal quincunx of four standard Portuguese laurels, clipped into the shape of mushrooms, and a domed *Phillyrea angustifolia*.

Planting within the knots is varied year by year, but typically might include larkspur, antirrhinums, nigella, lupins, aquilegia and amaranthus; whenever possible, varieties dating from the early 1700s are used. Within the walled garden are espaliered apples and pears, and fan-trained plums, peaches and apricots, at their glowing best on the NGS opening day in September.

The idea of controlling nature is essential to this most restrained of gardens. The hedges and topiary are tamed by being clipped into shape, while the natural flow of water is held still within the canals.

More exuberant is the garden at Coton Manor in Northamptonshire. It is very much a family affair, and three successive generations of Pasley-Tylers have made inspired use of the seventeenth-century manor house's natural setting amid wide views, and of the abundance of water on the site. The stone house, covered in spring with purple wisteria, is the focus of the garden, with walls supporting roses and shrubs, and terraces lined in summer with colourful pots. The garden was originally laid out in the 1920s by Ian Pasley-Tyler's grandparents, and was further cultivated from the 1960s by his parents, Henry and Haroldine. Haroldine was a friend of Valerie Finnis and her husband, David Scott, both respected horticulturalists of the period, and many of the unusual and interesting plants that still flourish in the garden came from their nursery.

Henry Pasley-Tyler's retirement in 1968 put the garden on a new footing, with two gardeners being employed full-time. This gave the couple the confidence to open regularly to the public, initially for the Red Cross and the local church, and then, from 1978, for the NGS, in which Haroldine became involved. Those were years of rapid change. The Pasley-Tylers dug out ponds in a field below the garden, and, in the style of the time, introduced exotic birds, such as Emperor geese and cockatoos (many of them in cages).

The Pasley-Tylers' son Ian and his wife, Susie, took over the running of the garden in 1991, continuing to open for the NGS and receiving their silver trowel, to mark twenty-five years of opening, in 2003. They, too, have put their mark on the garden by creating a rill and bog garden, and by establishing a wild-flower meadow in 1994. Boundary fences have been removed to incorporate the top field into the garden, and, although the cages have now gone, birds remain important to Coton. Visitors strolling round the

Opposite
In late April and May, the 5-acre (2-ha.) Bluebell Wood is an ocean of blue beneath a lofty canopy of unfurling green beech leaves.

Right
The Holly Hedge Border slopes down from the house with planting that includes delphiniums, roses, campanula and nepeta in high summer.

Right, bottom
Pots decorate the parapet of the terrace, along with clouds of red and white centranthus, *Alchemilla mollis* and blue hardy geraniums.

garden will encounter varieties of free-ranging
ornamental duck, teal and even flamingos.

Holly and yew hedges frame the lawns and
herbaceous borders that slope down from the
house. The luxuriant borders are planted to
provide interest throughout spring, summer and
autumn, with the main Midsummer Border a sea
of blue nepeta and delphiniums, and the crinkly
pink damask poppy *Papaver orientale* 'Patty's
Plum'. Another of Coton's glories is the water
garden, supplied with a constant flow of water
by the spring-fed main pond. The season there
begins with a bank of snowdrops and hellebores,
followed by a blaze of spring planting, including
tulips, azaleas, lysichiton, euphorbias, persicaria,
alliums, rhododendrons, hesperis and geraniums.
In late April and early May the Bluebell Wood
comes into its own: 5 acres (2 ha.) of soft-blue

The golden stone of Coton
Manor looks as magical on a
snowy day as it does in summer
sunshine. The house is seen
here from the pond at the
bottom of the main lawn.

The rill, which runs through the orchards, is one of the improvements that Ian and Susie Pasley-Tyler have made to the garden at Coton Manor.

English bluebells (no Spanish invaders allowed) beneath a lofty lime-green canopy of youthful beech leaves.

The woodland garden is full of interest from the first flowering of snowdrops in February, through the spring glories of hellebores, white narcissus, erythroniums, trilliums, anemones, violets and pulsatillas, to the cool summer planting of ferns, hostas, acanthus and fatshedera.

Ian and Susie Pasley-Tyler have built up a nursery and established a garden school for amateurs wishing to extend their gardening knowledge. The garden itself provides plenty of scope for lessons on planting, design and maintenance. The Pasley-Tylers have also continued to enhance the planting, benefiting from the sound foundation laid down by their predecessors. They recently overhauled the old rose garden, where many of the roses were suffering from replant disease. They were removed from four central beds and replaced with campanulas and lilies for July, and agapanthus, perovskias, sedums and salvias for September.

If the first NGS visitors from 1978 returned to Coton today for a May opening, they would undoubtedly notice many changes. But they would still remark on the garden's tranquil beauty, rich planting and abiding sense of peace.

1980–99
Village Variety

Leslie Geddes-Brown

The National Gardens Scheme has been praised for the fine work it does – not least the raising of millions of pounds for charity – but its work in inspiring the nation's gardeners has perhaps not had enough recognition. During the 1980s and 1990s a positive decision by trustees persuaded the County Organizers to discover and encourage smaller gardens in towns and villages. A by-product of this decision was that visiting gardeners were able to relate to the gardens they were seeing, in a way they could not have before. These were not lordly acres to be visited by sightseers, but real gardens worked by real people like the visitors themselves. Hence they were inspirational and educational as well as enjoyable. Not only has NGS patronage given encouragement and enthusiasm to people who open their small gardens, but also it has had a ripple effect with inexperienced gardeners. Many of those who open their smaller plots have noticed, over the years, that younger people, new to gardening, are making increasing visits.

Austin Lynch and Tim Culkin have been opening their garden, Millgate House in Richmond, North Yorkshire, since the early 1980s, and they find the changes to visitors to be striking. Visitors are more knowledgeable and more interested in the names of plants and where they can be obtained, and labelling has become much more important to them. Austin and Tim have even produced a garden guide, which explains what they have done to the garden and the techniques they have evolved.

Austin and Tim themselves were not very knowledgeable at the start, but over the years they have planted the steeply sloping ⅓ acre (0.1 ha.) plot so that there is barely a hint of the earth beneath. The lower garden was a vegetable plot when they first moved in, and the beds higher up were rectangular and filled with plants that liked the dry, light soil. The soil has been improved and the plants pruned to allow more light through; in 2012 the last remnants of lawn were replaced by gravel. Tim says that, after three decades, he thinks they have at last got to grips with the land.

The garden concentrates on roses, ferns, clematis and hostas (of particular interest is the treatment of slugs: a weekly spray with Sluggit). But what really put it on the map was that, in 1995, it won the *Daily Mail*/Royal Horticultural Society (RHS) National Garden Competition. The judges called it 'a sophisticated study in both the manipulation of spatial concepts and planting design. Roses perfectly integrated with a totally rounded planting scheme.' The garden was in the national consciousness; when it next opened, queues formed outside the wooden door to the street and thousands of pounds were raised for charity.

Austin believes that the NGS has done great missionary work and has much influence. He notices that the visitors are getting younger, and that there is a much wider range of styles in *The Yellow Book* than previously. Tim adds that the scheme encourages those who particularly want to

Opposite, top
A Celsiana damask rose flowers beside the coach house at the end of Millgate House garden.

Opposite, bottom
Rosa 'Constance Spry' flowers above a compact yellow juniper.

Right
The severe brick of Richmond's Norman castle is a fine foil for the lush planting at Millgate.

*Visiting gardens is the best way to discover
new plants. It's riveting in a nosy way,
stimulating in a creative way and inspiring
in an 'Isn't Britain fantastic?' way.*

Sarah Raven, gardener, writer and broadcaster

The prolific rose against the wall of Millgate House is 'Buff Beauty'.

learn, by showing them combinations of plants they can imitate, for example.

This famous garden has now returned the compliment to Richmond. The town gave it a sensational backdrop beyond its grey stone walls: the ruins of an eleventh-century castle poised above the often turbulent waters of the River Swale. Millgate House is now one of six major tourist attractions in a town that is only beginning to realize its potential. Visitors have come from Japan, and one party even turned up en route from Glasgow to Edinburgh, making the detour specially to see Millgate. The garden even helps local nurseries by listing plant suppliers.

Now, this charming garden opens every day, with special days allotted to the NGS. As Tim Longville wrote in the *Country Life* summer gardens special of 2002, it is 'a virtuoso, miniature version of a grand country-house garden. A paradise in God's own country.' There is nothing to compete with its sophistication and sense of relaxation within one of Britain's most attractive market towns. If this garden can stay hidden among the cobbled streets of Richmond, tucked in between electrical shops and pubs, it makes one wonder what other secret gardens exist in our high streets.

Sun House, on the main street of Long Melford in Suffolk, was a runner up in the same *Daily Mail*/RHS competition, and shares many of Millgate's characteristics. It is small; it is hidden behind a sixteenth-century town house in an attractive village; it is surrounded by high walls of brick and flint.

Its former owner, Maureen Thompson, who now gardens in the nearby town of Lavenham, remembers how poor a state the garden was in when she bought the property in 1981. The garden was full of old prams, bicycle wheels and buckets, and largely covered in ground elder. She and her husband dug up the ground elder, sprayed everything with glyphosate weedkiller and left the garden alone for six months. Next, it was planted to look good from the house. Then, in the early 1990s, they bought a tiny piece of land to make the 'secret garden'. To do so, she had to sell her collection of antique glass. She moved on in 2007,

but the garden is still opened for the NGS as one of a group of three in the village, by its new owners, Lord and Lady Dixon-Smith.

The garden was praised by the *Daily Mail*/RHS judges for providing colour and interest all year round: a wealth of tulips, euphorbias and hellebores in spring, then alliums and hostas, followed by delphiniums and lupins. Maureen Thompson found that visitors related to it because it is more difficult to create a small garden. There is no room for anything to hide, and the gardener must be very selective. Luckily, she has always enjoyed gardening, because it became a daily task – often starting at 5 am in summer. It was a labour-intensive garden, but not a tyranny for her, and her closely planted style arose partly because she wanted things to seed themselves. March, April and May were the difficult months, after which maintenance and pruning had to be carried out.

Below
There is nowhere to hide problems in a small garden. But distractions, such as this exuberant fountain at Sun House, are essential.

Opposite
The secret of making a small town garden look bigger is to hide the perimeter. At Sun House, the owner uses dozens of climbers, mass colour in the foreground and stately trees.

Opposite
Maureen Thompson covered the walls of Sun House with rambler roses, preferably pink, and more than 100 clematis for an exuberantly lush effect. Scent was another priority.

Above
A small town garden needs a censored colour scheme. Here, silver *Pyrus salicifolia* 'Pendula' overhangs groups of softly coloured perennials. Even the statue is a perfect match.

In common with Millgate, this town garden uses the surrounding walls as much as the flat areas inside them. The walls are clothed with climbing roses, honeysuckle, purple vine, ivy and – a master stroke – more than 100 clematis plants, which provide huge variety and flower from spring to autumn. Another special feature of Sun House is the emphasis on flowery scents from the old-fashioned roses, lilies, honeysuckle and jasmine; the fragrances are trapped in the garden by the high walls. Add to that the careful control of colour and it is easy to see why it has become such a popular garden to visit. Maureen originally refused to have orange in the garden, but she became gradually seduced by its assertive colour after her sister gave her a collection of crocosmia, and they are now in a special bed with deep-red foliage to take off the brightness. Bright red, however, was banned as not being restful.

Another haven is Island Hall, in the main street of Godmanchester in Cambridgeshire. The imposing house, which dates from 1749, is set close to the street behind a wall and a courtyard, but the gardens at the back are astonishing. The whole area is filled with history: one garden boundary follows the line of Ermine Street, a major Roman road; another is the Great Ouse on its way to the Wash. Between the main garden and the island from which it takes its name is a Saxon mill race. Beyond Island Hall's 2 acres (0.8 ha.) is Portholme, a 226-acre (91.5-ha.) water meadow filled with wild flowers in spring, with the song of larks and fine sunsets as extras. The diarist Samuel Pepys walked here in the seventeenth century and admired the milkmaids at work, and a hundred years later Portholme became a fashionable racecourse. It was later a cricket pitch and, in the early twentieth century, a landing spot for the aeroplanes manufactured in nearby Huntingdon.

Equally interesting is the fact that Island Hall is now owned by the interior designer Christopher Vane Percy and his wife, Lady Linda, since Vane Percy is the great-great-great-great-grandson of the first of his family to live at Island Hall. Vane Percys acquired the property in 1804, and the family stayed there until Christopher's second cousin sold up to the local council in 1958, depressed by the state of the building, which had been divided into fifteen flats. The ruined garden was covered with Nissen huts.

The garden today gives no clue to its sad past. One of the main features, the eighteenth-century Chinese Chippendale bridge over the stream between the main garden and the less formal island, was restored in 1988, using old photographs from *Country Life* to get the details exact. An eighteenth-century cupola was restored in 1995, again with the aid of old photographs. However, the ornate Victorian gardens, destroyed

Water, from the turbulent Great Ouse to placid streams, is an essential feature at Island Hall.

Christopher Vane Percy, an interior designer, takes as much care of the bones of the winter garden as of the face of the summer garden.

during the Second World War, have not been reproduced. Instead, an elegant lawn, only dotted with fine trees, sweeps down to the water. The island beyond is now a civilized wilderness, the cultivation carefully concealed. Vane Percy cites the art historian and landscape designer Roy Strong, saying, 'we don't have to resort to flowers', and takes it as a compliment when people compare the garden to a field.

It is not remotely like a field, of course. It is like a peaceful green runway that launches the eye into the historic views beyond. It is easy to forget the busy street only yards away, for meadows stretch to the horizon and the designer has carefully avoided anything that might stand in the way of the views. This has meant great discipline. Since the 1980s the Vane Percys have carried out a project every year. A part-time gardener is employed to trim the hedges, and a thorough tidy-up is done in

Christopher Vane Percy likes to vary the grass heights of the lawns. 'I like some a bit fluffy', he says.

Old photographs were used to restore the Chinese Chippendale bridge between the main garden and the island.

May, when everything is neatly clipped. Work is always in progress: a new avenue of Princeton elms now leads the eye to the water meadow, and a Victorian tennis court is being re-created.

In June and July Vane Percy mows the grass on the island to varying lengths, for a soft look. The wide lawn that slopes gently from the garden door of the house is also of mixed lengths: fine grass for croquet and slightly coarser grass for the rest. The croquet lawn is mown in careful diagonal stripes, while the rest is stripe-free. The island is as carefully tended, although it pretends not to be.

Vane Percy's idea for this green garden is that it be idyllic and 'a bit fluffy', but there is little fluffy about it. Instead, it is a designer's garden par excellence, every bit of it so right as to seem inevitable. It could be a high-street garden if Buckingham Palace could be described as a town garden – but Island Hall is better.

Croft Hall in County Durham almost qualifies as a high-street garden, albeit a very grand one. The Palladian house, painted a deep sienna shade of dull orange more usually found in Tuscany, stands back from the road in Croft village, but is very much part of it. The straight drive runs for about 76 yards (70 metres) through a simple garden notable for its lavender hedges, but nothing leads the visitor to expect the garden at the back of the house.

The Chaytor family has lived here since the early 1200s, and the house, although apparently Georgian, has traces of Tudor architecture. The garden was laid out only between the wars, and even now is in a constant state of change, but it is timeless.

There are 7 acres (2.8 ha.) in all, but far more Chaytor land surrounds them and is put to exceptionally good use. It comes as a surprise that,

Below
The garden at Croft Hall is designed gradually to fade into the rural landscape from more colourful planting near the house.

Opposite, top
The garden's basic layout follows the plan of the designer Thomas Mawson in the 1920s.

Opposite, bottom
The classical temple and its surrounding pond were made in the 1950s.

after the eighteenth-century formal front garden, at the back of the house is an ancient rural setting. The landscape has very cleverly been kept simple: from the windows at the back is a clear view over a flat lawn planted with nothing but lollipop hawthorn trees, which lead the eye out over the garden and, via a ha-ha, to the landscape beyond. In the adjoining field three horses graze as elegantly as they would have done 300 years ago. The lollipop hawthorns are cleverer than they seem, as the gaps between them are reduced further away from the house, for a false sense of perspective to make the lawn seem longer.

Much of the credit for the layout belongs to the designer Thomas Mawson, whose drawings for Croft Hall are still in the house. The design was created in the 1920s but, although much of the work was never done or was greatly adapted, the owners have retained its basic simplicity and formality, as befits the setting. At one side a small Palladian rotunda temple is mirrored in a pond, both dating from the 1950s. At the other side of the main lawn is a tennis court, ably hidden by a strikingly disciplined yew hedge. It is cut in scallops, and in front of its dark barricade is a bed closely planted with brilliant red tulips and nothing else. Wild yellow tulips, which spread by tubers underground, fill all the wild, grassy areas. Similarly, at the edges of the land at the front of the house, lawn gives way to long grass and trees, studded with semi-wild flowers, including honesty.

The current owners are Trevor and Kate Chaytor Norris, who proudly say that they had more than 200 visitors to their NGS opening in 2011 – there were just seventy when the garden was first opened. Their gardener, Robin King, has noticed a change in the visitors, who used to come from the village to amble round the garden. Now they come from much further afield, and generally make straight for the plant stall.

Despite its position in the village, Croft Hall is still a hidden gem. Its eighteenth-century

landscape is in keeping with the house, and its mown lawn is edged with wild flowers and large forest trees. This leads the eye inevitably to the rolling parkland beyond, with nothing else in sight. The cut yew hedges and little temple emphasize the effect. Yet, in the shelter of the main house is a formal, square herb garden, a large walled vegetable garden and sheltered courtyards. The buildings of the courtyards are painted in the same dark orange, their paintwork a soft green.

In the case of fine country houses with several acres of land to play with, design is far more crucial to success than is planting. Without the bones, the foreground loses structure. Indeed, the plantsman's problem is that it is all too easy to make a garden fussy. Of course, it is less fun to be restrained, but in such cases it is essential. Good design, like good bones on a face, endures longer than a careful choice of plants.

Sir George Sitwell visited hundreds of Italian gardens, all of which greatly influenced his nineteenth-century designs for Renishaw.

George Plumptre wrote about the gardens at the Sitwell family home in *Country Life* in 1994: 'The greatest challenge confronting any garden is the passage of time ... the gardens of Renishaw Hall in Derbyshire are a remarkable example of continuity, whereby the original design and major features all survive as the framework for harmonious embellishment added in recent years.' The siblings Edith, Osbert and Sacheverell Sitwell have always been celebrated, but the achievements of their father, Sir George, have perhaps been unfairly ignored. Disliked by his children for his rather eccentric character (he invented a small pistol for shooting wasps), he was responsible for the design of Renishaw's gardens, which, in 1994, had almost reached their centenary.

Sir George designed the gardens in 1895 when he was thirty-five, and after he had visited hundreds of Italian gardens, to which his own owe everything. Clipped yew hedges, statues, fountains and steps leading to vistas, along with great attention paid to

the uniting of garden and house within the landscape, contribute to one of the best Italian-influenced gardens in Britain. In 1909 Sir George described his garden philosophy in *An Essay on the Making of Gardens*: 'The garden must be considered not as a thing by itself, but as a gallery of foregrounds designed to set off the soft hues of the distance ... As the house must be related either by harmony or by contrast to the surrounding scenery, so the gardens should be in sympathy with them both.' Visitors today can appreciate how he transformed a corner of Derbyshire into a Tuscan garden by emphasizing these points. Even under snow the design is evident and powerful.

The main view from the house is of a wide lawn with, at its end, fine statues of Neptune and Diana at each side of a flight of stairs. They face away from the house, looking towards a large formal pool. Beyond this is another pair of statues, the Giants, also on either side of a flight of stairs, looking out over the surrounding park with a large

lake at the bottom. The whole is controlled by yew
obelisks now fronted by herbaceous borders and
ancient urns planted with flowers.

In 1909, the year he wrote his *Essay*, Sir George
bought a ruined castle in Tuscany: Montegufoni,
at that time was home to 300 Italian peasants. He
spent the next fifteen years restoring both house and
garden before moving there permanently in 1925,
and this may be why the bones of Renishaw's gardens
still exist basically unaltered, although softened by
later planting. Visits to Tuscan gardens convince the
visitor of the importance of Italian garden design,
even in a northern landscape, and so Renishaw
was an important influence on later British
designers; as much so, perhaps, as La Gamberaia,
close to Florence, where (as at Renishaw) intri-
cately formal design, statues and long vistas are
combined with woods and plain lawns.

The gardens at Renishaw were made in Sir
George's eccentric fashion, although today he
might be regarded simply as a perfectionist. Lawns
were raised and then lowered, until he felt they
were at the correct height, and lakes were dug and

Renishaw, designed in 1895
and unaltered for decades,
became an important
influence on later garden
designers. It is 'a remarkable
example of continuity', says
George Plumptre.

then re-sited to find the position that was exactly right. He imported statues, two of which are attributed to Caligari, and truly believed that unemployment in his Scarborough constituency (several counties away) would be helped by importing labourers to dig the 17-acre (nearly 7-ha.) lake. He rejected the planting plans of Gertrude Jekyll as too colourful; indeed, Jekyll has no place in this formal Italianate garden.

Sir George's grandson, Sir Reresby, and his wife, Lady Sitwell, have eased this austerity with plantsmanship, putting in climbing roses, clematis and a rose garden, and planting the surrounding woodland. Their work has added English garden touches to Italian formality. As George Plumptre wrote in 1994, 'The recent additions make Renishaw a garden of rare all-round quality, a joy to both garden-design enthusiasts and plants-men.' This is thanks to Sir George, Sir Reresby and Lady Sitwell; the famous siblings can claim little credit for Renishaw's beauty.

Left
Although later, softer planting, such as this cosmos, has been introduced, the design of Renishaw has been altered very little.

Below
In common with many Italian gardens, Renishaw introduces changes of mood with contrasting planting.

Opposite, top
Fenton House's formal lollipops of holly mirror the symmetry of the architecture. Agapanthus softens the view.

Opposite, bottom
Low shrubs lean out over gravel paths, but are kept severely disciplined.

We have already seen Croft Hall, which owes its serenity to Italian Renaissance garden design, and where the creators wanted a little bit of everything in just a few acres, as well as simplicity and formality. Fenton House in Hampstead, surrounded by the mansions of the rich and famous, and with spectacular views and a steep site, manages all that plus a historic orchard. The land surrounds the late seventeenth-century house, which is owned by the National Trust. Visiting grandees would have arrived via one of two entrances to the south and west; tradesmen came in at the bottom level and had possibly the best introduction to the garden. While the main entrances are designed with symmetrical yew topiary or a formal avenue of *Robinia pseudoacacia*, the tradesmen arrived through a vegetable garden and a charming 300-year-old orchard of twisted apple trees, three of which have still not been firmly identified. Others — 'Egremont Russet',

Left
Naturalized bulbs in the orchard are a delightful welcome to a London spring.

Below
Fenton House manages to combine symmetry and informality. The clipped hollies form a foreground to variegated pyramids.

Opposite
Fenton House Cottage (top) is at the bottom of the main garden. The prolific vegetable garden, with its adjacent orchard (bottom), has lettuces, spinach, beans and marrows, as well as decorative poppies.

'Lord Lambourne' and 'Ribston Pippin' — are espaliered along the gravel paths. The vegetable garden is still planted with chard, fennel and beans alongside impressive compost heaps, and there is a tiny herb garden. An old-fashioned Victorian greenhouse complete with iron gears and fretting to cover the underfloor heating is actually a reproduction.

The head gardener, Andrew Darragh, is comparatively new, having arrived in 2011 after ten years at Kew Gardens. His brief is to keep the garden as it is while filling up gaps in the planting. The box, damaged by blight, is being replaced, and there is a three-year management plan for the orchard. In the longer term, he would like to renovate the rose garden, to give height with roses on pillars and to underplant with such herbaceous plants as geraniums. He plans a late spring garden to prolong the season from March to September. Unlike most gardeners, he has to work with a committee, which has to agree to any plans.

Fenton House must be one of London's best oases, and is unlike all other London gardens, which are flat and rectangular. Its apparently simple design is actually quite complex, and on three levels, inviting the visitor constantly upwards and providing surprises, variations and vistas.

Nor does the garden of Jack and Elizabeth Lambert in Islington conform to the London pattern, the usual rectangle with walls 2 metres (6 ft) high, where gardeners try to hide the boundaries, the flatness and the unwillingness of grass to grow on London clay. The nineteenth-century house is at the end of a terrace, and the garden not only links to the building itself but also curls round the front and the boundaries. At its end is the New River (complete, in 2012, with moorhen's nest and chicks) with, beyond the water, a much-used public walk.

The garden at 37 Alwyne Road is flat but not a rectangle; indeed, it is hard to describe its shape, as the river ignores straight lines (although it is not a river but a seventeenth-century watercourse designed to bring water to the city from springs outside London). The garden has been cunningly designed so that its borders are hard to see, and the banks of the river beyond have been

Below
High hedges and clipped box at 37 Alwyne Road create structure, while colour comes from carefully chosen perennials.

Opposite, top
A garden conservatory, almost entirely private in the centre of London, is surrounded by a carefully planted garden.

Opposite, bottom
The house has views over the New River, which is here no longer part of London's water supply but remains part of a much-loved park, the New River Walk.

incorporated into the view, so the plot looks much larger. At any time of day, people wandering along these banks seem to be in the garden, a fact the Lamberts enjoy, except when dogs menace the baby waterfowl. There are also numerous squirrels in the overhanging trees.

In 2012 the Lamberts celebrated the twentieth anniversary of the opening of their garden for the NGS. It is large for London – about ½ acre (0.2 ha.) – and has a special area for potting up plants for sale on NGS opening day (queues are a regular feature), and another for a diminutive garden shed and compost heaps.

It is as near to a cottage garden as London gets, although the artlessness of the planting is superficial. There is a blue bed, currently filled with bluebells, cyclamen, *Allium cristophii* and camassias, and a silver bed over an old Anderson bomb shelter planted with cardoons and *Onopordum*. One of Elizabeth Lambert's policies is to use large plants as well as small, so the scale is cleverly varied.

The straight line along the boundary with Alwyne Road is broken by cutting the clipped yew into arbours and wider columns known as soldiers. A large yew on the lawn is clipped into a long spiral.

The garden is not allowed to rest on its laurels, and to celebrate the NGS anniversary the Lamberts constructed a conservatory at the back of the house, looking out on to a brick-floored patio full of topiary in pots. From here they can enjoy almost complete privacy and are surrounded by the garden, which has also been designed to be seen from the three upper floors of the house, including the kitchen. The view takes in not only the garden but also, in the distance, the spire of St Mary's parish church and a small octagonal pink building, a remnant from the time the Marquess of Northampton was lord of the manor (Alwyne is a Northampton family name). Also new in 2012 was a green garden of cut box in a geometric pattern (something that might inspire gardeners with nothing more than a bedsheet-sized space). Elizabeth is also planning 'a bad taste garden' full of the likes of French marigolds, since she finds it boring being tasteful all the time.

As have many of the owners whose gardens first opened in the 1970s and 1980s, the Lamberts have noticed that visitors have become younger and better informed. Although Islington house prices keep young buyers at bay, people come from many different areas to be inspired. They want to find out which plants will do well in London and how to cope with slugs; even owners of flats with nothing but window boxes can get ideas here.

The constant changes and the obvious enjoyment of the gardeners at 37 Alwyne Road account for the fact that this is one of the most popular gardens in the area. The Lamberts' problems are with queues and plants selling out rather than too few visitors – an excellent position to be in.

Mark and Sue Frost (number 7 Ambrose Place, Worthing; right) were asked to a garden meeting the day they moved in; neither had gardened before. Peter and Nina May (number 12; right, centre) have been at Ambrose Place only since 2010, but are already captivated. Most gardens are the same size, but the gardeners' inventiveness means that none is like any other (bottom).

The same applies to the famous Ambrose Place gardens in the centre of Worthing in West Sussex. This is an extraordinary story of how open gardens can become famous and, indeed, bring tourism into an area. It all started in 1984, when Mary Rosenberg at numbers 1 and 2 was persuaded by a friend to open her garden. She is now in her nineties, but the garden still opens and is immaculate. From these small beginnings, an average of twelve or thirteen gardens in the terrace now open (a huge feat, since people move on and their successors have to be persuaded to take part).

The houses are white-painted Regency with delicate ironwork balconies and porches, and were built by Ambrose Cartwright (who must have been pleased with his work, since he named the terrace after himself). They date from 1814–24; the odd one out is number 14, which was designed by another local man, John Biagio Rebecca.

Mary Rosenberg at 1 Ambrose Place (left) is a founder member of the openings, which began in 1984. Her house was once a vicarage. Alan and Marie Pringle (number 10; below): 'We invested heavily and it was two years before the garden opened. We are all very proud of being part of the NGS.'

Opposite
Tim and Fiona Reynoldson (number 3) knew about the NGS before they moved in. 'I like to remember where every plant has come from', Fiona says.

The terrace is listed Grade II. All houses have rear gardens similar in size to those in London, 80 ft (24 metres) long and the width of the house. But, unlike in London, each house has a front garden across the narrow street. These vary from parking spaces with greenery to lush planted areas. The houses each have a tiny square of garden alongside their gates and many have climbers – especially wisteria – reaching up the ironwork.

The back gardens are equally diverse, and that is why the terrace opening has been such a huge success. In a single small street the visitor can be inspired by gardens ranging in style from English cottage plots to spiky exotic jungles with all sorts of clever perspective ideas thrown in. Number 9 is a Provençal garden with a long rill and water spouts; number 10 (one of the finest, owned by Alan and Marie Pringle, the current organizers) takes inspiration from the Alhambra in Spain, with bottle brushes, palms, cacti and cypresses;

and number 12 is a cottage garden with terracotta pots, hollyhocks and a gazebo. Others have candlelit bowers for evening drinks; ponds for tadpoles, dragon- and damselflies; long wild-flower-filled lanes (actually paths leading from garage to back lane); and, in one instance, a garage that doubles as a cold frame by having a roof of transparent corrugated plastic. Fitted in beside the car are propagating trays, cuttings in pots and bags of compost. All this can be seen for (in 2012) a single £5 ticket. In 2006, when fourteen gardens were opened, 864 people came to visit and more than £4500 was raised for NGS charities. Since 1984, the terrace has raised a total of £88,000. On its twenty-fifth anniversary, in 2008, it raised more than £12,000 and made £1500 in plant sales. The year 2013 will be its thirtieth anniversary.

Another reason Ambrose Place is so success-ful and popular has to do with its organization. For my visit, Marie Pringle arranged a trip around half

the gardens, and a file of press cuttings from past years. She runs the opening scheme with a mixture of charm, determination and democracy. My press pack included a feature from the *Daily Telegraph* gardening section and seven pages from *The Times* magazine in 2008.

Equally importantly, this is not just a terrace of gardens that open for charity; it is a club of neighbours who get a social fillip from their work. The grandchildren of Sue Swanborough at number 6 have filled her garden with their own sculptures, and there was a garden sale of teddy bears found in charity shops. Christopher Middleton, writing in *The Telegraph* in 2005, wondered if living in the terrace might be a bit too neighbourly, but Mollie Stewart (number 11, and a founder member) says the residents are not always borrowing cups of sugar from one another. It is simply a sociable street. At the end of the great Open Day, full of adrenalin and enthusiasm, all the gardeners meet for a barbecue at Ambrose Villa, a larger house detached from the terrace. They talk about gardening and are already planning the following year's opening.

Above
Derek and Anna Irvine (number 9) 'quickly got carried away by the enthusiasm', and 'really enjoy opening', they say.

Opposite
Two different looks in Langford gardens: cottage-style exuberance at Bridgewater House (top), with massed herbaceous planting; and the Kemps Yard water feature has blue and white *Iris laevigata* and a miniature yellow waterlily. Roses are 'Eden Rose' and 'Belle Vichyssoise'.

Village openings have the same cameraderie, and there's no example more obvious than that of Langford in Oxfordshire, helpfully within David 'Big Society' Cameron's own constituency of Witney. This beautiful village of honey-coloured Cotswold stone is composed of fine early houses of some size, with cottages and a burgeoning council estate. It seems far bigger than the 300 inhabitants. It is even more astonishing that twenty-six of these houses opened their gardens for the NGS in 2012. Nine have been opening since Langford joined the scheme in the 1990s.

As in the case of Ambrose Place, the Langford village joint opening has had the benefit of an efficient organizer (now officially retired), David Range. He worked on the scheme – which, he admits, has its own way of doing things, such as not opening every year as the NGS would like – for ten years. He still spends a great deal of time organizing the hanging of the signs that direct visitors to this hard-to-find village. In the 1990s

visitors used to come in coaches, and the opening was a social event with a drinks party in one of the larger houses. Some days attracted more than 800 people and raised in excess of £4000, and the openings always raise between £2000 and £3000 for the NGS's charities. The gardens open only every second year to give the owners a chance to replant or carry out repair work.

The smallest gardens are 'London sized', and the largest about 2 acres (0.8 ha.). Owners vary from City bankers to Bob Stacey, who is nearly ninety years old and has a council house with a large garden and a pond full of koi carp. He gets letters thanking him for showing people round,

and begins his gardening year on Boxing Day, when he starts propagating plants for sale. Two other council houses also open.

David Freeman is at the Old School House, which he once shared with the royal couturier Sir Hardy Amies. It was Sir Hardy who transformed the old school playground into a garden so sumptuous that it merited a section in David Hicks's book *Cotswold Gardens* (1995).

Teas, plant stalls and a flower festival in the Grade I-listed St Matthew's church are organized by the villagers and, to make Langford Gardens Open Day a really special event, the bells are rung and there is usually live music or morris dancing.

The Old Vicarage, Langford, has colourful waterside planting of drumhead primulas and pelargoniums in stone urns. There are goldfish in the pond.

Anyone who believes the British are reserved should take a look at the private gardens listed in The Yellow Book. *Passion rules — from a royal retreat to a humble village garden made mostly of banked earth and African marigolds. I wouldn't want to live with either, but I love the devotion that has created them. On the other hand, I would happily live at the late Sir Hardy Amies's garden in Langford, Oxfordshire.*

Jane Owen, Garden Editor of the *Financial Times*

The low, white house and barely hardy planting give Cornish Trebah a touch of the Caribbean.

The crucial point about the gardens that open for the NGS is their great variety. So, we can jump from a council-house garden in an Oxfordshire village to a 26-acre (10.5-ha.) exotic landscape leading down to the Helford River in Cornwall. Although Trebah was put on the map by the Foxes of Falmouth, a family of garden-makers and plantsmen in the later nineteenth century, it did not open for the NGS until 1983, three years after it was acquired by Major and Mrs Tony Hibbert. Major Hibbert is now in his nineties, and his garden is run by the Trebah Garden Trust.

This is a garden of superlatives. *Gunnera manicata*, which, in an ordinary garden, might rise to 5 feet (1.5 m) high, is big enough at Trebah to behave like a herbaceous tree. There is room to walk under its huge, shady leaves. The tree ferns are no less majestic. Robert Pearson, in an article for *Country Life* in 1990, recorded other imposing trees: a Monterey pine at 106 feet (32 m) tall,

a winter's bark (*Drimys winteri*) at 46 feet (14 m) and a *Magnolia campbellii* at 42 feet (12.8 m). Three Chusan palms are the tallest in Britain.

The whole garden slopes steeply down to the estuary in a series of pools, ponds (one containing giant koi carp) and rivulets, a total of ¼ mile (0.4 km) in length. The head gardener is Darren Dickey, who has been at Trebah since 2002 and has made many changes. He removed nearly all the *Rhododendron ponticum* (no loss) and added masses of evergreen azaleas with white, pink and red flowers. He has also added an acer glade, planting forty different varieties. Their lovely bare stems gleam throughout winter – coral, red, shiny and peeling – and they include *Acer palmatum* 'Beni-kawa' and *A. shirasawanum* 'Autumn Moon'. He has planted 70,000 snowdrops and 60,000 cyclamen coum, which glow in January, and from April there is a sea of colour with candelabra primulas, arums, astilbes, hostas and

Opposite
The Helford estuary is an essential part of Trebah's complex planting: a calm stretch of water punctuating the lush gardens.

Above, left and right
Trebah is a very successful mixture of native and exotic species. The Chusan palms (above, left) make an architectural statement against a background of luxuriant planting.

other damp-loving marginal plants. There is even a 2½-acre (1-ha.) valley given over to hydrangeas and a forest of echiums.

Among the huge collection of trees and shrubs – about 1500 were recorded when Pearson was writing in 1990 – are varieties from China, Japan, Chile and Australia, taking advantage of Trebah's microclimate. However, although old accounts suggested that Trebah was the warmest garden in Britain, safe from frosts, Major Hibbert found that many plants succumbed over the years, especially in 1987 when a howling wind and temperatures of 5°F (-15°C) killed off bamboos, two *Rhododendron sinogrande* and a giant, 124-foot (37.8-m) *Eucalyptus ovata*. Then, as every gardener knows, nature is always on the prowl: fine plants die, but

new ones take their place. This is why, after three decades of opening for the NGS, there is always something new to see at Trebah. This spectacular Cornish garden is open for the NGS all year round, hence the importance of dash and colour even in November and February. As if that were not enough, visitors can enjoy a private beach on the estuary; and, considering the steep paths, the Trust has two motorized buggies for the use of the less mobile.

These ten gardens all first opened between 1980 and 1999, and I chose them because they celebrate the enormous variety of size, style, planting, climate and enthusiasm that has come to typify the gardens that open for the NGS. Nothing is like it anywhere in the world.

2000–12
Garden Visiting in the New Millennium

Christopher Woodward

A wild garden by Henk Gerritsen blurs the outlines of an Arts and Crafts-style design at Waltham Place in Berkshire.

The first decade of the twenty-first century has been perhaps the most splendid of great garden-making since the Edwardian age. A newly rich generation has invested in house and garden at the same time as the inheritors of old estates have revealed a sudden relish for contemporary interventions; strikingly, the modern master-pieces we shall see at Scampston and Boughton, at Waltham Place and Broughton Hall have each been commissioned by established families in the context of a wider restoration.

When Hugh Johnson edited the magazine *The Garden* in the 1970s (he reflects from Saling Hall, a great *Yellow Book* favourite; see pp. 134–37), it seemed as if private gardens were doomed; at a very basic level, fewer and fewer owners could afford to pay a gardener. The change he has witnessed has been nothing less than a Renaissance of British gardens. But, better still, a hundred years ago very few of the new gardens featured in *Country Life*'s iconic photographs were accessible; now, through the National Gardens Scheme, we can enjoy this investment of money, time and horticultural and design skill.

Strikingly, the client also has a wider choice of garden designers than ever before, although at the same time the medium continues to be one in which a non-professional can compose a master-piece. You cannot, after all, write the history of modern garden design exclusively through the work of professional designers, as that would be to exclude Beth Chatto, Christopher Lloyd and Derek Jarman. Two recent, acclaimed memoirs, *The Morville Hours* (2008) by Katherine Swift and *The Garden in the Clouds: Confessions of a Hopeless Romantic* (2010) by Antony Woodward, describe, beautifully, the process of intelligent and patient self-education in horticulture and in the making of a place.

But perhaps this Renaissance of garden-making is also a consequence of a wider and more alert audience, debating gardens through

magazines and books but, above all, through the act of visiting. The modern garden owner has the confidence to replace a walled garden planted with Christmas trees (as at Scampston; see pp. 190–94) or a 'Capability' Brown vista boxed up with Nissen huts for battery hens (Lowther Castle, Cumbria) because he or she is confident that sufficient visitors will come for a day out. During this period the NGS has not just kept up with the pace; it has also broadened its role. A *Yellow Book* opening has become a conclusive moment in the making or restoration of a garden.

The decade has also been rich in new design ideas – so rich, in fact, that it is a challenge to a contemporary critic. It is very hard to see what the fundamental movements in design and style will turn out to be: one is too close up, like a child squeezed into a wardrobe of clothes, and with such a choice that a writer can pick an outfit to suit his argument. But garden visiting is a continued influence on the design and making of gardens: every new garden is born in a visit to another.

'I have one question: Why?' asked a local grandee at the public unveiling of the new walled garden at Broughton Grange, Oxfordshire, commissioned from Tom Stuart-Smith in 2000. It was Stuart-Smith's first large garden, and perhaps the first masterpiece of the new millennium. It is also – and this explains the grandee's question – 'a little like an aircraft carrier parked in a field', as the designer puts it. A Victorian rectory stands smugly in hayfields above the Sor Brook, a tributary of the Cherwell. The new garden is huge, higher up the slope, and bears no visual or physical relationship to the house.

The designer explains the project in 'Attachment and Separation', his first essay on his own work (*Garden Museum Journal*, vol. 25, 2011), although we must guess at the mysterious client. The only clue is that on his return from business

At Broughton Grange in Oxfordshire, the garden is entirely separate (and invisible) from the house. The slope is divided into contrasting areas, with a pool at the centre.

trips, however late, he sits down and relaxes not in the house but within the walled garden. It is not quite a walled garden, however, as it is designed to be open to views of the country on the south and east. Inside are three terraces, whose planting changes from level to level: hot and dry Mediterranean species in shallow soil at the top; a lush, waist-high meadow; and, at the bottom, a parterre of box, its inter-cut design a magnified slice of the cell pattern of native trees. In the centre of the middle terrace is a void, not a structure: a reflective pool of water, with the occasional flash of self-absorbed koi carp.

In 2011 the London College of Garden Design asked writers and designers to select a favourite modern icon and argue its case to an audience. The writer Ursula Buchan chose Broughton Grange, and the unpacking of its complexities happily took up forty minutes. What is striking on re-reading Stuart-Smith's own essay is his awareness of an audience for his design, although

There is one garden in England that I visit almost every year and have done ever since I first went there as a student. There aren't many flowers to speak of; nor are there many visitors, which is both wonderful and inexplicable, since it is arguably the finest surviving early eighteenth-century garden in England. I've seen it in snow, rain, fog and sun. Where is this magical garden that draws me back again and again? You may be able to guess, but perhaps by not revealing, a little of that tantalizing thrill of the unknown is preserved for a moment, like the apparently closed garden gate that seems to deny access to some hidden retreat of unimagined beauty.

Tom Stuart-Smith, garden designer

The parterre on the lowest level of the garden at Broughton Grange echoes the cell pattern of native trees in its outlines of box (*Buxus sempervirens*).

that audience cannot be as neatly categorized as the client, the grandee or the subscriber to *Gardens Illustrated*. Garden design is, in part, self-reflection: a part of every designer is his own visitor, in the same way that every novelist is also his most truculent reader. This is how Stuart-Smith explains it:

> In James Wood's book *How Fiction Works*, there is an account of a single paragraph of Henry James's *What Maisie Knew*. Wood shows how James moves between three different perspectives in his description of the young Maisie, so that one has the sense of oscillating between several psychological positions, and perhaps being in several places at the same time. Of course a garden is a rather more solid

thing than a fully drawn Jamesian heroine, but as with a character there is a constant interplay between the individuality of the subject and its context.

This garden has a strong and purposeful progression combined with vivid detail and native trees and hedges sheltering exotic plants; it is also open to the wider landscape, like a novel about an individual family in which from time to time the world marches past or shouts by the open sash windows. More deeply, however, a kind of peer review is implied in this passage: with a client so purposeful but so receptive, and with such an open site, and budget, it was Stuart-Smith's chance to respond to his mentors, his education and his travels.

Scampston Hall in North Yorkshire first opened for the NGS in 1927 and continues to do so. Today, the visitor to the walled garden sees a contemporary insertion by Piet Oudolf, who inaugurated the millennium by winning Best in Show at Chelsea in 2000, in a collaboration with Arne Maynard. Oudolf is perhaps the most influential planting designer in the world, in large part owing to the phenomenal popularity of the High Line in New York: 1½ miles (2.5 km) of planting on an elevated railway rescued from demolition and transformed into a park in the sky; and enjoyed by 4 million people every year.

There have been Legards at Scampston since 1690, and they have employed such designers as Charles Bridgeman and Lancelot 'Capability' Brown. In 1998, the interior of the house restored and open to the public, Lady (Caroline) Legard turned her attention to a walled garden in which Christmas trees grew for sale, and wondered whether there was a modern designer with the distinctive vision of a Brown. She had read about the German school of habitat planting, led by such figures as Karl Foerster and Ernst Pagels, and next came rumours of a Dutchman who fused that scientific and ecological knowledge with an artist's sense of composition. Oudolf, Caroline read, was lecturing at Bury Court in Sussex, where the plantsman John Coke had commissioned Oudolf's first garden in the United Kingdom. The next year Oudolf came to Scampston and began a project that divided the garden into nine 'rooms' using yew, box and beech. The plants distinctive to his gardens – salvias, astrantias, asclepias – were propagated in greenhouses on the estate for him to inspect. As the Legards explain Oudolf's philosophy, plants must 'grow gracefully, live gracefully and die gracefully'. The geometry of the evergreen structure is just as striking as the colours and textures of the perennials and their seed heads.

To the younger designers restless for change, Oudolf's vision was a challenge to traditional English gardening, with its accepted division into zones of 'ornamental' and 'wild', and a standard of maintenance that required dead-heading, staking and a flawless beauty concentrated into a short May to July season. His photographs of the garden show the beauty of dead seed heads in spider-webbed September or frosty skeletons in February. For Coke, English planting in the 1990s seems parochial in retrospect, in its 'palette' and its reliance on 'the random snaky hose and the traditional mixed border'. The book *Dream Plants for the Natural Garden* (2000) by Oudolf and Henk Gerritsen introduced new colours of astrantia and salvia, and a wilder, spikier and more vigorous silhouette.

Reading old magazine articles, unrolling faded faxes and conducting interviews, it is evident that in the 1990s there was a strong desire for 'something new'. John Brookes of Denmans in West Sussex (see pp. 112–15), *enfant terrible* still, declared himself bored with a cycle of period revivals, whether Arts and Crafts structure or the spinning colour wheel of Gertrude Jekyll. (And why – a question to which we shall return – does the country house continue to be the apex of a designer's aspiration, rather than the small garden, or the park?) Brookes asked what was new out there; 'I have seen the future, and it's Dutch', declared the horticultural writer and photographer Derek Fell.

The 'Dutch Wave' was not a conscious, shared movement but rather a coincidence of individuals who rebelled at the artificiality of traditional horticulture. They were connected by a reconsideration of the gardener's relationship with Nature, and a curiosity to observe the natural movements and relationships of plants in gardens. These individuals are impossible to lump together. The tag 'old hippy' might be applied

The Gardens of England

(amiably) to Henk Gerritsen (see below) and the late Rob Leopold, a philosopher who set up a business selling native flower seeds picked from the garden of a ruinous farmhouse. Leopold wrote most angrily of the trays of begonias and geraniums bright as plastic stacked in garden centres, and tried to articulate a manifesto of movement, spontaneity and freedom. Ton ter Linden tried zookeeping and gymnastics before becoming a painter and then beginning a garden in the small town of Ruinen, remembered by the writer Stephen Lacey as 'the most electrifying planting I had ever seen'. Its borders were composed with the colours of a Monet painting and so intense that from April onwards there was no space to weed or tinker; Ton ter Linden became a spectator of horticultural fireworks. (Ter Linden is exceptional in that he does *not* visit other gardens.) Oudolf, the son of a hotelier, fell into a fascination with plants during a summer job in

a nursery, and, in his twenties and newly wed, set up as a landscape contractor. Two children later, he and his wife, Anja, bought and renovated an old farmhouse at Hummelo, near Arnhem, and opened a nursery. In the grounds they began to experiment with a new range of plants.

One of the first visitors was Gerritsen, an artist and conservationist, who had begun a garden at the family home of his partner, Anton Schlepers. At Hummelo the Oudolfs hosted 'garden days', with packets of Leopold's native seeds pegged up to decorate the polytunnels, stalls of plants and books, food and wine, and discussions late into the night. Flicking through the Oudolfs' photographic albums, one begins to see English faces: Coke; Tania and James Compton, the writer and botanist; Christopher Lloyd and Penelope Hobhouse side by side on a bench; Lacey and the camera of the BBC's *Gardeners' World*; Rosie Atkins, whose periodical *Gardens Illustrated* transformed the public's expectation of gardening magazines with its beautiful and spacious photography. Changes in garden history are the consequence of the chemistry achieved by open gardens: as when Oudolf strode up to the nursery at Bury Court and sparked an immediate friendship with Coke, or when Caroline Legard persuaded her husband to drive for four hours to hear a lecture. Whatever innovations in media we have seen, it is travel, talking and friendship that continue to jolt garden history forward.

At Scampston, sculptural wooden seats by Piet Hein Eek are shaded by *Phellodendron chinense. Molinia caerulea* subsp. *arundinacea* 'Transparent' planted in blocks is constantly on the move.

The borders at Waltham Place are filled with repeating clumps of calamagrostis and *Persicaria polymorpha*, the giant bistort. A pergola beyond is covered in rambler roses.

Perhaps the most radical commission in a British country-house garden was the result of a coach trip. In September 1999 Strilli Oppenheimer of Waltham Place in Berkshire joined a group tour to Dutch gardens, including the farmhouse of Priona, inherited by Schlepers from his parents and built on the last patch of native woodland in a grid of intensive post-agriculture. Gerritsen had not wished to make a garden there: his interest was in botanizing in natural habitats, and as a young man he had written with visceral anger at the suburban gardener's obsession with ordering Nature and arranging colour in the manner of a Victorian watercolourist. Priona was his experiment in creating a genuinely natural garden. It was opened to the public in 1986, and Gerritsen assembled a collection of letters from visitors complaining at the cabbage leaves munched by butterflies, unmown lawns and flowers that turned out to be

parsnips. Strilli, who visited at the end of a hot summer, remembers a fellow traveller on the coach tour, the writer Diana Ross. For Gerritsen the drought was just a new challenge in his dialogue with Nature, and, leaving the puzzled group to explore the parched, half-dead garden, Ross discovered him 'alone, gently separating out a tangle of carrot seed heads to expose a group of lilac-coloured colchicums' (*Garden Museum Journal*, vol. 24, 2010).

In Gerritsen, Strilli discovered the collaborator she had been looking for: a man who combined her spiritual belief that we do not own Nature – a plant's colour and growth is a miracle to be observed, not an ingredient to be appropriated for a designer's 'palette' – with a patiently earned expertise in botany. First she took him to her family's garden at Brenthurst Place in Johannesburg; that tempted him to Waltham Place, which opened for the NGS in 2010

to celebrate the centenary of its acquisition by the Oppenheimers.

At Waltham Place Gerritsen created a garden unique in Britain for the play between bold, sculptural topiary and exuberant, naturalistic planting. A formal garden had been laid out in the 1930s in an Arts and Crafts style, with ponds and brick pergolas; within this rectangularity Gerritsen set loose an exploding caterpillar of topiary, surrounded by drifts of stunning planting that flows with colour until late autumn. British writers have focused on the ivy gnarling the pergola, the ground elder and the bindweed trumpeting its flowers on trellises erected for the purpose. Soon, however, the visitor notices that it is not a 'wild garden' at all: Gerritsen's vision requires a greater intensity of attention and plant knowledge than a traditional horticultural master-piece. And season by season one is more and more deeply moved by the joyousness of plants.

The pergola (pictured on p. 195) and formal lily ponds (opposite) were retained by Gerritsen at Waltham Place. Behind the undulating box topiary (right) are drifts of grass beneath a lookout tower.

'Henk knew more about plants than anyone I have ever met', recalls Strilli; he was able to let loose such spontaneity precisely because of his knowledge of their behaviour. He was dying of AIDS during the making of the Waltham Place garden, and Strilli dispatched her gardener, Beatrice Krehl, a Swiss who had studied with Gerritsen's mentor Mien Ruys, to study beside him in The Netherlands and, in doing so, transmit his ideas to posterity. Waltham Place continues to startle, as in the balustraded terrace outside the drawing room: plants spike up through the paving, a few steps from the polished plate glass of the facade.

In 1994 Stephen Lacey and the landscape designers Tim Rees and Brita von Schoenaich organized a symposium at Kew Gardens on habitat planting, and presented to a sold-out auditorium the ideas developed in Germany over many decades. Attendees recall a sense of the ground shifting beneath their feet as speaker after speaker showed slides of drifts of self-determined planting. Professor James Hitchmough of the University of Sheffield was one of two British speakers, and his planting – created with his colleague Professor Nigel Dunnett and the designer Sarah Price – of the Queen Elizabeth II Park on the site of the Olympics in east London is the spectacular flowering of ideas that germinated in the 1980s.

The second British speaker was Beth Chatto, who represents a distinctively English approach to ecological planting, a highly personal synthesis of the groundbreaking studies of her husband, the late Andrew Chatto, the paintings and horticulture of her second mentor, Cedric Morris, and the underlying toughness of her personal landscape. Indeed, her gardens at Elmstead Market in Essex (see pp. 128–31) became a place of pilgrimage for such Europeans as Oudolf, the designer Jacqueline van der Kloet and Cassian Schmidt, director of the Hermannshof, Weinheim.

One day Beth received a fan letter from a nine-year-old boy called Dan Pearson. Pearson's precocious knowledge of and enthusiasm for plants were such that later, during a scholarship in Israel, he would take a bus into the countryside the day before the Sabbath. At midnight the bus would stop, wherever it might be; Pearson would pick up his knapsack, get off the bus, and begin to study whatever plants the dawn revealed.

Pearson is unusual among the top flight of designers in his interest in small town gardens and scruffy urban spaces, but he intersects with our story of country-house innovation at Broughton Hall in Yorkshire. In 2001 the owner, Roger Tempest, invested in the transformation of a 2-acre (0.8-ha.) Victorian walled garden into a centre for small rural businesses, commissioning the architect Michael Hopkins to design a cafeteria for it, a contemporary glass pavilion plinthed on a grass mound. Forty businesses are located in the service buildings outside the walled garden, which has become a communal space for more than 500 workers. Pearson's challenge was to plant a garden that would absorb and refresh the workers, whether they wished to chatter at lunch tables or lose themselves in thought. Paths lead through beds of tall perennials, curved to slow the pace. Beside the cafeteria are low enclosures built with drystone walls, inspired by the sheepfolds of the county. Pearson noticed a tradition in which trees are planted in the centre of sheepfolds, to shelter livestock. At Broughton Hall an apple tree is planted in each enclosure, so that employees can pick and munch the fruit at lunchtime.

The estate at Boughton House in Northamptonshire is an unfinished work by the eighteenth-century landscape designer Charles Bridgeman.

In 2004 the Marquess of Dalkeith (now the Duke of Buccleuch) invited the landscape architect Kim Wilkie to Boughton House, near Kettering in Northamptonshire. The two men walked up the truncated pyramid built by the 2nd Duke of Montague as the base for a mausoleum, which was never constructed. Some 800 yards (730 m) of formal gardens march back to the house, which was begun by the family at the end of the seventeenth century; as are Chatsworth and Petworth, it is a house expressive of the power and prodigious wealth of the nobility created by Charles II after the Restoration. For the greater part of its life it has played a secondary role to the family's estates in Scotland, and for the curious art historians of my generation it acquired the reputation of a shuttered treasure house, with half-lit masterpieces in tapestry and leather to be admired in the gloom by a lucky few. Today, the house and gardens are not only restored but also the cradle of an innovative educational programme that includes the garden and park.

A formal garden was commissioned from Charles Bridgeman in the eighteenth century but never completed; indeed, the old plans studied by Wilkie annotated the space between house and pyramid as 'hurried over'. The site had never been resolved. 'What would you do?' asked Lord Dalkeith. 'The simple question on the hill was an intense moment,' says Wilkie, 'and I am not sure what answer was expected, but one came to me in a flash. Rather than make a rival mount or competing structure, I replied: "Why not go down rather than up?"'

The result was the excavation of an inverted pyramid 164 feet (50 m) square and 23 feet (7 m) below the water table, with an Escher-like grass path descending to black water. The project is named 'Orpheus' after the tragic hero of Greek myth, who descended into the Underworld to plead for the return to life of his beloved Eurydice. At the opening the gold-chained Mayor of Northampton led a procession of the glitterati of the gardening press down the ramp in what seemed to be a procession to a very English Hades.

The project might be seen as a work of conceptual art, and Wilkie cites the sky sculptures of the American artist James Turrell as an inspiration. Grass mounds and curves are the most recognizable signature of Wilkie's work, but, as his book *Led by the Land* (2012) reveals, these are simply the most visible expression of the designer's ideas about the identity of place. He reminds us that Alexander Pope spoke of 'the genius, and use, of the place' ('Of the Use of Riches', *Moral Essays*, 1731–35) – and that we too easily drop the word 'use'. Wilkie's work is distinguished by an interest in the economy of landscape, whether cattle-grazing or food-growing, and the imprints we make. Orpheus fuses Greek myth and English ecosystem; it was made in less than a year by the core estate staff, using their knowledge of the local springs and beds of clay.

The project was also named after Orpheus as the god of music, and the opening inaugurated a programme of musical performance. As strings tuned, punts ferried guests across Bridgeman's canalscape in an image suddenly reminiscent of the prints by Jacques Rigaud of the entertainments at Stowe and Chiswick in the 1720s and 1730s. By this date the great gardens of Britain were open to the public on a structured basis: an inn for domestic tourists, a guidebook to buy and a Stranger's Gate at which the visitor would be met by a gardener or his boy (see p. 12). In 2012 the National Trust completed a visionary restoration of the inn built at Stowe between 1717 and 1721, and re-created the visitor experience enjoyed by the eighteenth-century public.

This was the culmination of a growing interest in understanding the historical visitor experience. For a long time the garden historian has known that a visitor's sketch or letter can unlock a puzzle in a lost landscape; in the 1980s this converged with a new academic movement named 'reception theory', in which responses to art galleries and novels were analysed as experiences to be studied in their own right – independently, that is, of the original intentions of the creator. Personal

reactions are valuable precisely *because* they are personal. A ruin might prompt a poet or painter to make their own work of beauty or fragility; or we can discover an underlying cultural zeitgeist: studying the growth of domestic tourism in the eighteenth century – as opposed to the Grand Tour – casts new light on the nation's burgeoning patriotism.

One British garden in particular is critical to any such analysis of modern garden visiting: Sissinghurst (pp. 67–69), which in 1980 became the first National Trust garden to introduce timed ticketing (the number of visitors had risen from 25,000 a year at Vita Sackville-West's death in 1962 to 180,000). In *Sissinghurst: An Unfinished History* (2008), Adam Nicolson, Vita's grandson, was prompted to reflect on why and how we visit gardens. He argues that the key factor in Sissinghurst's rise in popularity was the widespread success of *Portrait of a Marriage* on its publication in 1973: its revelation of Vita and her husband's secret love lives sold in great numbers, lost him several old friends and widened the audience far beyond the field of horticulture.

Today Sissinghurst is a cult (a 'literary-lesbian-hortico-aristocratic' one, according to Adam in his book). At the end of each season its gardeners point to the 'admiration patches' on the lawn, where people have stood to enjoy a rose or wisteria. 'The public come for privacy', Nicolson concludes: we each want to be alone in Vita's dream world, to be the person who discovers the key to the secret garden. Indeed, the more selfish and personal our sense of discovery is, the further our imagination travels. We enjoy the bustle and gregariousness of garden visits, but many of us duck down a side alley, tiptoe into a potting shed to sit alone in the nostalgic mustiness, or wait for the people in front to move out of the viewfinder.

The attraction might be snobbery, or perhaps there is a motivation deeper than that which draws us to a garden with the intimacy of Sissinghurst.

At Boughton House, the Mount (seen top left, from the house) is mirrored by Kim Wilkie's 'Orpheus', a spiralling grass path leading to an excavated pool.

Sissinghurst, Nicolson points out, lost its 'innocence' as soon as Vita rattled the tin for the NGS in 1938. Very quickly, his grandparents became conscious of an audience, and, he argues, imagined their reaction at each step. Sissinghurst as 'sleeping beauty' is an illusion in which Vita and her audience were happily complicit.

Antony Woodward's *The Garden in the Clouds* is a classic story of a couple – Antony and his wife, Verity – packing up successful careers in London to begin a new life in the countryside, having fallen in love with Tair-Ffynnon, a derelict, concrete-rendered farmhouse on a breathtaking (and axle-busting) site 1300 feet (400 m) up on the shoulder of a mountain between England and Wales. But the twist is that he sets himself the challenge of making from scratch a garden that will be judged good enough for *The Yellow Book* – and the next year's, at that. The story has a happy ending: the County Organizer smiles, 131 visitors make their

way up the track, £700 is raised and every crumb of cake is consumed.

The Garden in the Clouds itself is an essay in the garden-maker's relationship with the expectations of friends, family and the public. Woodward quotes a friend's father, who asked – or stated – 'Where's the garden?' that first day. But he is too modest about Tair-Ffynnon. As at Derek Jarman's iconic garden on the shingle beach at Dungeness, an unforgiving site and a beginner's boldness have created something absolutely new, which feels absolutely right. The 'Infinity Vegetable Patch' is a drystone-walled enclosure on the edge of an infinite view; a poem by Edward Thomas is lettered on the side of the barn; above, giant box spheres roll through a meadow, with paths mown to imitate the tracks of giant snowballs.

Woodward concludes that he has made the garden that is in his mind: the remembered garden of his grandmother, an idyll from which he

The Garden in the Clouds in Monmouthshire is a product of situation and climate as much as human intervention.

was 'expelled' by its sale when he was five years old. Perhaps the gardener is forever re-making a lost paradise, he muses.

If you drive to Tair-Ffynnon for the next opening, you will pass very close to Meryswydden, where the grandparents of Sarah Price lived. Price was the designer of the moment in 2012, owing to her Gold Medal-winning garden for *The Telegraph* at the Chelsea Flower Show, and her collaboration with James Hitchmough and Nigel Dunnett on the site of the Olympics. She studied fine art at university before training as a gardener, a confluence expressed in a film she made with Ruth Parker to record four seasons in the life of the dying garden at Priona, filmed after Gerritsen's death. Her written reflections on her work lead back to her grandparents' garden: to 'a glasshouse full of tiny adiantum ferns and the smell of geraniums, peaches and fermented grapes in late September; a dark "dog" house full of clutter, with a dusty old ship's bell to ring; beehives in a secret, overgrown garden that was accessible only by a tunnel under the lane.' Explorations were checked only 'on *Yellow Book* days [when] I was allowed to help make the teas, but was instructed to stay out of sight' ('Garden Visits to Meryswydden', *Garden Museum Journal*, 26, 2012).

That childhood garden has changed, and revisiting is a troubling process of overlaid images, of disjunctions in scale and smell. But why *are* such gardens so critical to creative development? Most deeply, Paradise is rooted in Western minds as an enclosed garden – although its first expression was purely as an enclosure of pleasure: stone reliefs at Taq-i Bustan in Iran apply the word 'paradeiza' to the slaughter and consumption of wild boar within a walled space. Nevertheless, gardens evince a relationship between space and time that is uniquely potent to the adult imagination.

In 1949 the Dutch historian Johan Huizinga wrote a book called *Homo Ludens: A Study of the*

We all need fresh ideas from time to time, and visiting other folks' gardens is by far the best way of finding them. 'That's clever; we should try that', or 'I like that plant – what is it?' give us a shot in the arm. And then there is the joy of knowing that the responsibility for that garden – and for keeping it looking good – is someone else's!

Alan Titchmarsh, gardener, broadcaster and novelist

Play-Element in Culture, in which he argued that whereas for a child play is defined by spatial boundaries (the garden, the playground), for an adult it is limited by time. The busy adult sees the trip to the allotment or the football match as an allowance or gift of time, not of spatial freedom. Huizinga's purpose was to show that Western man lost the enchantment of play during the Industrial Revolution; the immediate consequence was nostalgia for lost childhood, as reflected in the Golden Age of children's literature in Britain, which began with Charles Kingsley's *The Water-Babies* (1863) and reached its apotheosis in Frances Hodgson Burnett's *The Secret Garden* of 1911. 'The Child began to be taken seriously, when the Man was forced to stop the same kind of delight in the world as he had done when he was a child', rhapsodized Huizinga. In *The Secret Garden*, Burnett captured an archetypal experience of garden visiting: personal discovery, solitude and invisibility coupled with a sense of security. Mary Lennox's first visit after her discovery of the key to an ivy-covered door also shows the complexity of our experience of time in a garden: it is a space in which the past (the swing, and the spot where her mother fell to her death), the present (the silence and stillness, broken only by the hops of the robin) and the future (the green tips of bulbs) are inseparable.

To an adult, the rarest gift is perhaps to be able to enjoy the present; for there are very few hours each week in which we genuinely 'live in the moment'. Perhaps it is a question of minutes, not hours. But in other peoples' gardens we are not preoccupied by maintenance, or fraught with competing demands or duties. We have no choices to make about the future (except, perhaps, which cake to eat) and the lawn does not trip us up with doubts about past decisions. Other people's gardens are, perhaps, the places in which it is easiest to experience the spots of sunlight that are absorption in the present.

Utopia exists in the future, Arcadia in the past, wrote W.H. Auden in a great, half-buried essay on, as it happens, *The Pickwick Papers* ('Dingley Dell and the Fleet', *The Dyer's Hand and Other Essays*, 1962). Why, he asks, did the book bore him as a child but delight him as an adult? *Pickwick* is not a book for twelve-year-olds, not because of any aspect of its content or language, but because it is a study in the Fall of Man. Mr Pickwick is an innocent adult, and children do not 'get' him because they have no understanding of innocence, argues Auden, and innocence, like Eden, is discovered only in its loss: 'to be no longer innocent, but to wish that one were, is part of the definition of an adult'. Adulthood is defined by the obligation to make difficult choices, and we become nostalgic for places and times when, we imagine, there was no need for such decisions, or

for sacrifice: childhood, holidays and, I suggest, being in gardens that are not our own. Read Auden's paragraph, think of a perfect garden visit, and see if it applies:

> Every adult knows that he lives in a world where, though some are more fortunate than others, no one can escape physical and mental suffering, a world where everybody experiences some degree of contradiction between what he desires to do and what his conscience tells him he ought to do or others will allow him to do. Everybody wishes that this world were not like that, that he could live in a world where desires would conflict neither with each other nor with duties nor with the laws of nature, and a great number of us enjoy imagining what such a world would be like.

Perhaps this also helps to explain why the great designers or makers of gardens are rarely inspired by their parents' garden, unless it was big enough for wild edges, woods or hidden, overgrown corners. Invariably, that garden is a grandparent's (as for Sarah Price and Antony Woodward), or belongs to the kind, wise neighbour described by Dan Pearson as his mentor in his book *Spirit: Garden Inspiration* (2009). Or it is a secret garden whose owner and their actions will always be mysterious.

Charles Rutherfoord, chairman since early 2012 of the Society of Garden Designers, plants 2000 tulip bulbs in his garden in Clapham, south London, in readiness for an NGS opening in April. His enjoyment is evident: for a designer signed up by private clients, on open day the garden at 51 The Chase becomes a stage. 'The great pleasure I have found is that visitors provide a spur to develop different parts of the garden so that there is always something new', he explains. 'Quite a few come back to see the garden either in a different season or to see the new parts.'

But there is a relationship between maker and audience that is unique to gardens. A tiny percentage of the audience at the theatre or at an art exhibition will have written a play or painted a picture. But the great majority of the strangers at Rutherfoord's gate will be active gardeners. That changes the relationship fundamentally: the audience is formed not of passive spectators but of active participants.

That participation has widened as the NGS has broadened the type of garden that opens to the public. John Brookes has repeatedly challenged us to 'move on' from our obsession with the country house as the apex of achievement and become lovers of public space and town gardens. We have not done that, as this chapter alone betrays. In addition, at the time of writing there is a perceived crisis in the standards of horticulture and maintenance in public parks, as a report commissioned in 2012 by the Heritage Lottery Fund from the charity Green Space confirms. Most immediately this is owing to cuts in public spending since 2009, although it can also be attributed to local authorities' preference for one-off capital projects with ribbons and plaques. More deeply, I wonder if our love affair with the private garden – and our embarrassment of choice – is a factor: if we are obsessed with Sissinghurst, we are unlikely ever to make a High Line.

The Gardens of England

Charles Rutherfoord's garden at 51 The Chase in London is planted in spring with tulips and wallflowers, underneath a laburnum tree.

The geodesic dome by Rupert Tyler at 51 The Chase is filled with succulents and subtropical plants, as well as sheltering seedlings.

The Queen Elizabeth II Park created for the 2012 Olympic Games will be the test of this doubt.

More positively, a great phenomenon of the NGS's most recent decade has been an exponential increase in the number of small town gardens open to the public. Cycling home to east London one day I noticed a yellow poster: four gardens in neighbouring streets would open that Sunday. My first glimpse of yellow balloons tied to railings led me to Chris Thow and Graham Hart's Victorian town house on Lansdowne Drive (part of the London Fields group opening). The garden is magical.

In 2006, Chris and Graham explain, the garden consisted of a lawn, neglected shrubs and a shed that appeared 'disproportionately large'. Now the shed has all but disappeared behind the huge plants with which Chris has filled the available space: black and green bamboos, tree ferns, banana plants, palms and paulownia. The layout is simple: a straight path cutting across a winding central walkway to produce quarters of unequal size. Two ponds have been dug out, and *Gunnera manicata* towers over the largest, which is populated by fish, frogs and newts. The achievement is that the size and density of the plants increase the apparent size of the place, and the visitor's immersion. A large mirror at the very end of the garden is the only trick that has been used to make it feel bigger.

Other types of garden have been increasing in *The Yellow Book* in recent years. An interest in allotments is a phenomenon itself; since 2007 the sale of seeds for 'grow your own' fruit and vegetables has outstripped that of seeds for flowers, and anecdotal evidence suggests that *Yellow Book* visitors to allotments go to collect practical tips (see photograph, p. 216). In Liverpool you can see a garden surrounding a tower block (York House Gardens, part of the

The Gardens of England

The garden at 61 Lansdowne Drive in east London is a lush, green enclave of tree ferns, bamboo and gunnera. Climbing hydrangea clothes a shed, while a mirror cunningly extends the view (bottom).

Garden Barge Square near Tower Bridge is an unexpected horticultural delight in the heart of the city. One boat-owner has even planted a tree – the yellow-leaved *Robinia pseudoacacia* 'Frisia'.

Sefton Park Gardens group opening), while London's Garden Barge Square is an archipelago of houseboats downstream from Tower Bridge; at the wrong time of day you recognize the ooze in which Bill Sykes sinks to his death. The architect Nick Lacey rescued the derelict houseboats as a community development, and created gardens on the boats and the rattling walkway that runs between them. It is a floating and tilting Eden, whose apples hang lower as the boats settle with the tide.

Kathy Gee, a poet and curator, joins her neighbours at an open garden day in her village in the Midlands; she has been struck by how vocal, animated and quick a garden audience is compared to that for art or museum. Her village will remain anonymous, because her observations should not be pinned to a single entry. She classifies visitors as follows:

Colour people: very visual, observing colour contrasts and harmonies. Sometimes they point out leaf texture and shape. Practical people: compost bins and potting area; where do you buy stone-faced pond liner? The horticulturalist: in search of specific plants, and always asks about the one you don't know (turned out to be *Lathyrus vernus*). The problem-solver: how do you deal with half the garden in permanent shade for half the year? The decorator, who notices the metal sculpture and the blacksmith-made verandah. The designers, who are interested in the shape of the garden, its curves and divisions, and where you would put the shed. Finally, the 'curious aspirant', who fancies living in the country, or a village, and for half an hour can imagine that this is their life, their garden.

In the summer of 2012 Tom Stuart-Smith's client at Broughton Grange was revealed in the press to be Stephen Hester, a highly respected executive who had been asked by the government to turn the Royal Bank of Scotland around after its bail-out with public funds. The anti-banker movement Occupy discovered that Broughton would be open for the NGS, and announced its intention to turn up and pitch camp within the walls. To Hester the right spirit was to continue, and the yellow 'Garden Open Today' posters stayed up. In the end it rained. The four anarchists who *did* turn up stayed in their car and waited for the rain to stop. It didn't, and they drove away. It is a very British postscript to a very British story.

Open Garden
Kathy Gee

Already there are strangers in the street.
Breakfast, dead head, trim and set;

admire the backlit circle ears of wood mice,
messy eaters. Sweep the courtyard,

check the garden pond for corpses. Take
a quiet moment at the gate.

Strangers pause and make a threshold sweep
to find their personal horizon,

pausing, wanting this to be the one.
Close your eyes and dream a while;

just take a string from here to there
and that's about what we could do.

Hosta rustle walls beneath the nest box.
Busy blue tits carry on

while garden owners talk of colour, roses,
compost bins and moss control.

They watch as couples plan a future, mothers
teach their daughters herbal lore

and how to cook the slow old way.
And, side by side with no eye contact,

friends say *look at that* to intercept
a point they do not want to answer.

They treat us like a gallery, except
you cannot fake a garden.

Beneficiaries

The National Gardens Scheme was founded in 1927 by the Queen's Nursing Institute to provide financial support for district nurses. Eighty-five years later the Scheme remains true to its founding principles by donating annually the great majority of funds raised at garden openings, to a selected group of nursing and caring charities. From time to time lesser amounts are given to other chosen charitable activities.

Since it began, the Scheme has donated some £40 million to nominated beneficiaries, of which nearly £25 million has been given since 2002. Its continuing support means that for most of its beneficiaries, it is the largest cumulative donor in their histories; this is the case with its founder, the Queen's Nursing Institute, and with its two largest beneficiaries, Macmillan Cancer Support and Marie Curie Cancer Care.

For many years the NGS has provided funding towards the National Trust's careership scheme, which trains future head gardeners to diploma and degree level in the specialist role of managing a large historic garden. In return, National Trust gardens open on certain days in aid of the NGS.

The beneficiaries of The National Gardens Scheme are:

The NGS has supported Marie Curie Cancer Care for more than fifteen years, raising a staggering £6 million during this time. This money raised enables the charity to continue to provide high-quality nursing, totally free, to give people with terminal cancer and other illnesses the choice of dying at home, supported by their families.

Help the Hospices champions the very best care for everyone facing the end of life. The NGS has supported us, and through our work more than 200 hospices, since 1997. Over the years, generous funding from NGS has supported a variety of programmes including training for hospice staff, equipment for delivering hospice at home services, hospice awards and national projects supporting clinical excellence.

The Queen's Nursing Institute campaigns for the best possible nursing care for patients in their own homes. Our community of Queen's Nurses leads by example, and we support practical projects in the community to improve patient care. We believe that skilled, professional and dedicated nursing should be available to everyone, where and when they need it

Carers Trust works to improve support, services and recognition for anyone living with the challenges of caring, unpaid, for a family member or friend who is ill, frail or disabled, or has mental-health or addiction problems. Ongoing support from the NGS has meant a great deal to carers over the years, and countless individuals have benefited as a direct result of its donations.

The NGS has been a partner of Macmillan Cancer Support since 1985 and is proud to be the charity's largest single donor. Raising in excess of £13.7 million, this has funded more than 140 Macmillan services, including clinical nursing specialists, financial advisors, dieticians, physiotherapists and counsellors, helping to make a huge difference to the lives of thousands of people affected by cancer across the United Kingdom.

Through Perennial, the NGS helps horticulturists who are facing difficulties. The NGS donation is invaluable to the charity's ongoing work to help individuals and families. The annual donation to Perennial for gardeners' children also enables ongoing support for families when one or both parents have died, and for children who are disadvantaged by other circumstances.

Index

Contributors

Elspeth Napier trained in horticulture at Wye College, and was editor of the Royal Horticultural Society and RHS representative for the NGS. Since retiring from the RHS she has helped to organize NGS garden openings in Kent and Warwickshire.

Catherine Horwood is a writer and gardener, and the NGS's Assistant County Organizer for Suffolk. She has written books and articles on a variety of subjects, including garden history, and was a specialist consultant to the exhibition *A Garden Within Doors* (2010) at the Geffrye Museum, east London. She gardens in north London and Suffolk.

Vanessa Berridge was the editor of *Country Homes & Interiors* magazine, and conceived, launched and edited *The English Garden*. Now a widely published freelance writer on gardening, gardening history and heritage subjects, she contributes to *The Garden*, *Homes & Gardens* and *Country Life*, among other publications. She gardens in London and Gloucestershire.

Leslie Geddes-Brown, former deputy editor of *World of Interiors* and *Country Life*, writes on gardening and interior design for the *Daily Telegraph*, the *Sunday Times*, *You* magazine, *Country Life* and, in the United States, *Garden Design* and *Town and Country*. She gardens in north London and Suffolk, where she opens her moated manor-house garden for the NGS.

Christopher Woodward is a writer, curator and architectural historian, and director of the Garden Museum in London. He was previously director of the Holburne Museum of Art in Bath. His first book, *In Ruins*, was published in 2001.

Picture credits

l = left; r = right; t = top; b = bottom; c = centre

© Alison Appleby: 20l; courtesy of Viscount Ashbrook: 55 (all); © Richard Bloom: 132; © Mandy Bradshaw: 141t; courtesy of Bramdean: 74c, b, 76–77; © John Brookes: 112–13, 114br, 115; © Leigh Clapp: 50, 51t, b, 90b, 91t, b, 92, 93; © Val Corbett: 37t, 38, 39b, 98–101, 148–51; courtesy of Cottesbrooke Hall: 70–73; © *Country Life*: 2–3, 10, 14l, 15l, 24, 27t, b, 33c, 33b, 36b, 41c, b, 42t, b, 43b, 46–47, 49c, b, 53b, 54t, b, 56, 57t, b, 58 (all), 59, 62b, 69cb, b, 75t, c, b, 78tl, bl, 90t, c, 117t, 138c, b, 152–56, 158, 159, 180, 182, 183l, r, 184, 186, 187t, b, 188, 189, 195–99, 201–203; © Carole Drake: 102–105; © Heather Edwards: 94–97; © F Stop Press/Renishaw Hall: 163, 166t, b; © Charles Francis: 48t, b, 49t; © Garden Museum: 13r; © Garden Museum/ photographer J.W. Packham: 17; © Suzie Gibbons: 211, 212; © Harpur Garden Library: jacket front, 6, 22, 43t, 45t, b, 108t, b, 109, 110, 111l, r, 116, 117b, 118t, b, 134–37, 142–45, 164, 165, 179, 181t, bl, br; © Gordon Hay: 171b; © Hestercombe Gardens Trust: 60 (all), 61, 62–63t, 64, 65t, b; © John Hinde: 217; © John Colley Photography, courtesy of Melbourne Hall Gardens: 26, 28–29, 30t, b, 31t, b; © Elizabeth Lambert: 170–72; © Andrew Lawson: 82–85, 114t, bl, 190–94; © Rosanna Lewis: 36t, 39t; © David Logan: 133; © Lovegrove Weddings: 20r; © National Trust: 13l, 167t, b, 168t, b; © National Trust Images: 138t, /Jonathan Buckley: 69t, /John Hammond: 12, /Jerry Harpur: 169t, b, /Paul Harris: 41t, /Nick Meers: 37b, /Stephen Robson: 139, 140, 141b, /Ian Shaw: 146, /Rupert Truman: 40, /Penny Tweedie: 66, 68, 69ct; Newby Hall collection: jacket back, 44; © Heiner Orth: 210; © Allan Pollok-Morris: 200; © Mark Potter: 176; courtesy of Ramster: 25, 52t, b, 53t; © Colin Roberts: 78r, 79t; © Jane Sebire: 214–215; © Shanah Smailes: 160–62; © Chris Thow and Graham Hart: 213 (all); © Nicola Stocken Tomkins: 8, 74t, 86t, b, 87t, 88t, b, 89; © Nicola Stocken Tomkins/The Garden Collection: 79b, 80, 81; © Grace Vane Percy (zooeye.com): 157t, bl, br; © Anthony and Penelope Warne: 32, 33t, 34–35; © Rachel Warne: 128–31; © Nigel Watts, courtesy of Lady Amabel Lindsay: 124–27; © John Whitaker: 106, 119t, b, 120t, b, 121t, b, 122t, b, 123t, b; © Jack Wilson: 21; © Antony Woodward: 204–209

The NGS and the publisher have made every effort to trace and contact copyright holders of the illustrations reproduced in this book; they will be happy to correct in subsequent editions any errors or omissions that are brought to their attention.

First published in 2013 by Merrell Publishers,
London and New York

Merrell Publishers Limited
81 Southwark Street
London SE1 0HX

merrellpublishers.com

British Library Cataloguing in Publication Data:
A catalogue record for this book is available from
the British Library.

ISBN 978-1-8589-4602-3

Produced by Merrell Publishers Limited
Designed by Alexandre Coco
Project-managed by Rosanna Lewis
Indexed by Hilary Bird

Printed and bound in China

Plant names have been checked against the Royal
Horticultural Society's Horticultural Database,
available at rhs.org.uk

Jacket, front
Renishaw Hall, Derbyshire
(see pages 163–66)

Jacket, back
Newby Hall, North Yorkshire
(see pages 42–45)

Frontispiece
Blickling Hall, Norfolk
(see pages 36–39)

Page 6
Coton Manor,
Northamptonshire
(see pages 142–45)

Page 8
Dunsborough Park, Surrey
(see pages 86–89)

Page 217
Kingsway Allotments,
Newton, Cheshire

Acknowledgements

We should like to offer our thanks to His Royal Highness The Prince of Wales, Patron of the National Gardens Scheme, for generously consenting to write a Foreword for the book.

We are also grateful to Joe Swift, President of the NGS, for writing the Preface, and to the authors of the book's main chapters: Elspeth Napier, Catherine Horwood, Vanessa Berridge, Leslie Geddes-Brown and Christopher Woodward.

Our thanks go, in particular, to the garden owners who kindly allowed their gardens to be featured on behalf of the NGS: Lord and Lady Ashbrook, John Brookes, the Brudenell family, the Duke of Buccleuch, the Buchanan family, Beth Chatto, Mr and Mrs T. Chaytor Norris, Richard and Lucinda Compton, Lord and Lady Dixon-Smith, Neil and Anthea Foster, Michael Galsworthy, Mr and Mrs Paul Gunn, Stephen Hester, Hestercombe Gardens Trust, John Lewis Estates, Hugh and Judy Johnson, Denise Kemp, Lord and Lady Ralph Kerr, Nick Lacey, Jack and Elizabeth Lambert, Lord and Lady Legard, Lady Amabel Lindsay, Alistair and Sheran Macdonald-Buchanan, the National Trust, Strilli Oppenheimer, Dominic and Stephanie Parker, Mr and Mrs Ian Pasley-Tyler, Perennial, Alan and Marie Pringle, Faith Raven, Nicholas Rothschild, Charles Rutherfoord, Alexandra Sitwell, Patricia Stout, Baron and Baroness Sweerts de Landas Wyborgh, Chris Thow and Graham Hart, Trebah Garden Trust, Michelle Upchurch, Christopher Vane Percy, Victoria Wakefield, Anthony and Penelope Warne, Mike and Gail Werkmeister, Antony and Verity Woodward.

We are grateful to the individual photographers, who are acknowledged on page 223, and to the National Trust and *Country Life* picture libraries. Our thanks also to all those who contributed quotations.

We should like to thank the NGS team, including Stephanie Fudge, Julie Knight, Elizabeth Milner and Wendy Morton; also, at Merrell Publishers, Hugh Merrell, who first suggested the book, Rosie Lewis, our patient, diligent editor, and Alex Coco, who produced the elegant design.